Professional Practice

A Handbook for
Interior Designers

Professional Practice

Ronald M. Veitch
Dianne R. Jackman
Mary K. Dixon

1990
Peguis Publishers
Winnipeg, Canada

Printed in Canada

Second printing 1996

Canadian Cataloguing in Publication Data

Veitch, Ronald M. (Ronald Miles), 1931–
    Professional practice

        Includes bibliographical references.
        ISBN: 0–920541–37–2

1. Interior decoration.   I. Jackman, Dianne R. (Dianne
Rose), 1934–   II. Dixon, Mary K. (Mary Katherine),
1936–   III. Title.

NK2116.V44 1990   747   C90–097055–3

Book and cover design: Pat Stanton
Illustrations: Scott Barham
Forms: Karen Diell

Peguis Publishers Limited
100—318 McDermot Avenue
Winnipeg MB R3A 0A2 Canada
1-800-667-9673

Foreword

A number of years ago, ASID forged a promotional campaign entitled "ASID means BUSINESS." It was a successful promotion, not simply because of its catchy slogan, but, more importantly, because the professionals who were practicing interior design admitted, by inaugurating such a campaign, that interior design was indeed a "business." To be sure, the initial thoughts behind ASID means BUSINESS were to promote ASID, to reinforce to its members as well as non-members that ASID was serious about what it was doing, and that by being involved with ASID one could reasonably expect to *increase* one's business as well as become more competent in the business of interior design. But what was perhaps not envisioned by the leaders of ASID at the time was that the slogan was far broader in its scope than merely focusing on ASID and the potential mutual benefits of membership.

It seems that there was a hidden meaning in the slogan, which recognized that interior design was more than the creation of beauty and the concentration on the health, safety, and welfare of the public. Indeed, interior design was and is, in addition to those more obvious attributes, a business. Big business! It has been documented by a number of various groups and publications that the business of interior design is in excess of forty billion dollars a year in goods and services in the U.S. alone. Forty billion!...with a "b"! That is **big** business.

To admit that interior design is big business, and to concentrate on those qualities, attributes, and skills that will make that business even bigger, and hopefully, easier, has been a slow process. Traditionally, those involved in the *creative* fields have been considered to be less *business-minded* than those practitioners of other professions. That critical position and view is probably justifiable when you consider that there have been many designers who, for whatever reasons, did indeed concentrate more on the aesthetics of a job than on the *accounting* of the job. There are, of course, hundreds of excuses: the "I can't be bothered with money" attitude...or the "They never taught me that in school" approach. Many designers have felt it beneath them to discuss money with a client. They would rather discuss the design solution. After all, they are *designers* not accountants. At times, it even seemed as though one would be considered less of a designer if a somewhat business-like attitude prevailed in daily activities. For some unknown reason, business awareness and acumen, to some, seemed to indicate a lack in the aesthetic realms.

Traditional mindsets are difficult to overcome. It is interesting to note that stereotypes occur with more traditionally recognized business people as well. How many times have you heard accountants or businesspeople flippantly, even apologetically, say "Sorry, I can't draw a straight line." They can't draw that straight line because society has dictated that for them to be businesslike, they must concentrate on the bottom line and leave the straight line up to those creative types. But, for designers at least, it seems that those traditional attitudes and hangups are changing; interior designers *are* becoming successful and businesslike.

Without question, when you see an interior designer of any reputation and success, if you look behind all the exterior trappings of his or her design abilities, you will find a person who is well organized and skilled in controlling and maintaining a good solid business, based on proven and stable business procedures. You will find a business person who is not afraid to discuss the financial arrangements with potential clients before entering into a job. You will find a business person who recognizes that most, if not all, of his or her clients are business people who expect and appreciate working with other professionals who are familiar with and practice professional business management. No doubt, you will find a business person who, after concentrating on his or her creative skills, has realized that in order to create a platform that will showcase those special talents, must devote an equal amount of energy and effort to honing good *business* skills as well.

Like anything, be it creativity or business, awareness and exposure are the best teachers. Learning the basics is essential. This book, *Professional Practice: A Handbook for Interior Designers*, offers an excellent source for such awareness. It provides an easy checklist of the myriad of details that starting and maintaining a successful design practice entails. It introduces the basic "jargon" of business that is so essential when working with other professionals. And perhaps most important, it provides an enormous amount of valuable information in an organized manner with a sense of wit and fun. That word "fun" may be the key to this whole discussion of creativity versus business. Designers, for the most part, have fun with design...and they think that there is no way that business can also be fun. Perhaps it is the fear of the unknown. Designers of today and tomorrow, armed with the information presented in this book, can take advantage of the big business opportunities that exist in a field that has every opportunity to be filled with fun and fantasy...as well as dollars and cents.

Charles D. Gandy, FASID
Past President ASID and Senior Partner, Gandy/Peace Inc.

Preface

Our objective in writing this book has been to bring to the attention of students the scope and complexity of the practice of the profession of interior design. Other books have been written about the design process and the development of creativity. We wish to expose the neophyte designer to the practical aspects of the profession, which, when understood and managed successfully, allow the designer to work creatively. Also important is the international commonality and wide-open horizon of our profession, offering unlimited scope and personal direction for the beginning interior designer.

Although *Professional Practice* has been designed primarily for the use of students, we believe that practicing interior designers will find it a valuable resource–"one-stop shopping" for a myriad of information vital to the practice of interior design.

This book has been made possible through long and varied practice, many years of teaching, national and international contact within the profession, continuing-education programs sponsored by the professional organizations, special lectures given by colleagues in the Professional Interior Designers Institute of Manitoba, publications of interior design associations, and the shared knowledge of many individual colleagues.

Contents

The following sample business forms can be found in the insert between pages 98 and 99.

Business Forms

Introduction

Every individual lives, works, and interacts within the built environment. To each of us, home is that important place where we find rest and renewal, appreciation and stimulation. For most of us there is a separate place for work where we are productive, efficient, and fulfilled. And all of us find places where we are entertained, educated, inspired.

Interior design is the only profession specializing in the creation of places to meet all of these needs. Through education and practice, designers cultivate their natural talents to become experts in the development of harmonious places to meet the aesthetic and emotional, as well as the practical, requirements of the occupants. They feel a social responsibility to affect the built environment in a positive way. By creating the spaces in which people live and function, designers may even affect the success or failure of their endeavors.

Good interior design is a cooperative effort. The client is always involved, and it is the client's emotional needs which must be met, and the client's activity which must be accommodated. Analyzing and interpreting the client's preferences and requirements, communicating and guiding the choices to be made (for there is never just one solution), and emerging with an aesthetically pleasing and functional space is a great challenge and an even greater accomplishment when done well.

Interior design is not an easy profession, and it is not a simple matter to attain professional status. The education is rigorous and time-consuming and is undertaken successfully only by those individuals who care about other people as well as have an interest in and appreciation for beautiful and functional spaces.

Understanding the inner workings of the profession is essential to the development of the interior design student into a caring, sensitive, professional—one capable of creating interior environments to satisfy both the users' practical requirements and their inner needs. Relating the course work contained in the various years of the program of studies to the differing phases of practice underlines the importance and relevance of what otherwise might seem unrelated experiences.

A program of studies is a network of interrelated and interdependent areas; so is the profession. Business,

Definition of an Interior Designer

The professional interior designer is qualified by education, experience, and examination to enhance the function and quality of interior spaces for the purpose of improving the quality of life, increasing productivity, and protecting the health, safety, and welfare of the public.

The professional interior designer
- analyzes client's needs, goals, and life and safety requirements
- integrates findings with knowledge of interior design
- formulates preliminary design concepts that are appropriate, functional, and aesthetic
- develops and presents final design recommendations through appropriate presentation media
- prepares working drawings and specifications for non-load bearing interior construction, materials, finishes, space planning, furnishings, fixtures, and equipment
- collaborates with professional services of other licensed practitioners in the technical areas of mechanical, electrical, and load-bearing design as required for regulatory approval
- prepares and administers bids and contract documents as the client's agent
- reviews and evaluates design solutions during implementation and upon completion

design, management, construction, and community involvement are all components. The number and international scope of professional associations and their involvement with legal and moral issues indicate that interior design is a major profession. All interior designers should know *about* their profession–as well as how to practice it conscientiously–and should work towards meeting the criteria outlined in the "definition."

Interior Design Services

The services performed by the professional interior designer are broad indeed, as may be understood by reading through the diverse activities undertaken by the designer during the course of a project.

Programming

- identifies and analyzes the client's and users' needs and goals
- evaluates the existing documentation and the condition of the premises, including furnishings and equipment, space allocation, and other attributes of the existing environment
- assesses the project's resources and limitations, both physical and financial
- identifies life, safety, and code requirements
- considers site issues, such as location and access
- prepares project schedule and work plan
- develops budgets for the interior construction and furnishings
- analyzes the design objectives and spatial requirements
- develops preliminary space planning and furniture layouts, and integrates the findings with knowledge of interior design
- determines the need for consultants and other specialists when required by professional practice or regulatory approval, makes recommendations to the clients, and acts as a coordinator
- organizes information for client discussion and approval

Design Concept

- formulates the preliminary plans and three-dimensional design concepts that are appropriate to the program's budget and that describe the character, function, and aesthetic of the project
- prepares image boards
- presents the conceptual design and preliminary cost estimates to the client for discussion and approval

Design Development

- develops and refines the approved conceptual design
- researches and consults with jurisdictional authorities regarding building and life safety codes, applicable health and liquor regulations, and so on
- communicates with specialists/consultants as necessary
- develops the art, accessory, and graphic/signage programs
- develops and presents for client review and approval the final design recommendations for space planning, furnishings, fixtures, millwork, and all interior surfaces, including lighting, electrical, and communication requirements
- refines budget estimate
- prepares a presentation to the client for discussion and approval, using a variety of media such as drawings, perspectives, renderings, color and material boards, photographs, and models

- prepares for client approval the working drawings and related schedules for interior construction, materials, finishes, furnishings, fixtures, and equipment
- coordinates the professional services of specialty consultants and licensed practitioners in the technical areas of mechanical, electrical, and load-bearing design and construction, as required for regulatory approval
- identifies qualified bidders
- prepares the bid documents, construction specifications, and furnishings specifications
- issues addenda as necessary
- collects and reviews the bids
- assists the client in awarding contracts

Contract Documentation

- administers the contract documents as the client's agent
- confirms that the required permits are obtained
- monitors the contractors'/suppliers' progress
- as necessary, issues proposed change notices, change orders, and so on
- conducts periodic site visits and inspections
- reviews and approves shop drawings and samples
- oversees the installation of furnishings, fixtures, and equipment
- reviews the invoices and issues certificates for payment
- prepares list of deficiencies
- makes final inspection
- prepares the equipment and maintenance manual
- monitors the project through the guarantee period
- completes the termination of contracts

Contract Administration

- reviews and evaluates the design solution after project completion
- if retained by owner, conducts a post-occupancy evaluation summary

Evaluation

In the end, the professional is an individual qualified by education and experience to design, specify, and supervise the development of functional, aesthetic, and cost-effective interior spaces and, in so doing, to have a worthwhile, satisfying, and well-paid career.

Introduction to the Profession

I

The Profession of Interior Design

Interior design as a profession has grown rapidly in both breadth and depth over the past three decades. It has become a full-fledged profession, involved in all aspects of creating the built environment–from researching and writing the initial program for the project, through creating the spaces, supervising the construction, and evaluating the success of the project after completion. Interior designers are educated to become creative professionals who analyze problems from many different perspectives; apply philosophies, theories, and results of empirical investigation; and synthesize and reshape information in the development of their design solutions. While new technologies affect the skills and knowledge required of interior designers and enable them to adapt to a changing world, designers also draw upon the lessons of history and the experiences of many cultures.

Education, Training, and Examination

Formal education is the first component in a sequence of preparation for professional interior design status that also includes entry-level experience (internship), and satisfactory completion of qualifying examinations.

An educational program provides a balance between the broad cultural aspects and the specialized practical content that is integral to the profession.

Programs of study vary depending on the publicly articulated goals of each institution, and they are housed in such administrative units as Architecture, Home Economics, Fine Arts, and Environmental Design.

Important to the formal education of an interior designer are implications of the health, safety, and welfare of the

public on design. These implications may be explored within the following areas of study:

- ▸ knowledge of anthropometrics and ergonomics
- ▸ proxemics and behavioral theory
- ▸ requirements for special populations, such as the disabled and the elderly
- ▸ interior construction and detailing
- ▸ lighting
- ▸ heating, ventilation, and air conditioning
- ▸ physical attributes of materials, installation methods
- ▸ building codes
- ▸ fire codes and life-safety requirements
- ▸ industry product standards
- ▸ business practices
- ▸ specifications writing for interior construction and furnishings

> ▸ *anthropometrics:* **the branch of anthropology that deals with measurement of the human body**
> ▸ *ergonomics:* **the scientific study of the relationship between human beings and their working environment**
> ▸ *proxemics:* **man's perception of social and personal space**

FIDER (Foundation for Interior Design Education Research) Standards and Guidelines require the studies listed above, among others, to be part of an accredited curriculum.

Entry-level experience is required for professional status and for full membership in the major professional associations. Licensing bills make specific experience levels mandatory for entry into a recognized profession, and codify the requirements for length of practice, proof of experience, and so on.

Full membership in the major professional associations also requires that individuals pass **qualifying examinations**. NCIDQ (National Council for Interior Design Qualification) administers examinations which are recognized throughout the United States and Canada. Exams include content in reference to the health, safety, and welfare of the public.

Interior Design Associations

Interior design achieved recognition as a profession in North America in the early thirties. At that time, the first professional associations were formed–in Canada, La Société des Décorateurs-Ensembliers du Québec (SDEQ) and in the United States, the American Institute of Decorators (AID), which later became the American Society of Interior Designers (ASID).

It is interesting to note that the SDEQ established a practice act in three Quebec locations as early as 1938, and required passage of a two-part examination that tested both residential and commercial design capabilities through written and design questions. The AID instituted a qualifying examination in 1966.

Currently, the associations may be classified as follows:

Associations in Canada

IDC–Interior Designers of Canada

Associations in the United States

ASID–American Society of Interior Designers
IBD–Institute of Business Designers
ISID–International Society of Interior Designers

Note: All of the professional associations above have international and overlapping memberships.

International Associations

IFI–International Federation of Interior Architects/Interior Designers
IDEC–Interior Design Educators Council

FIDER–Foundation for Interior Design Education Research
NCIDQ–National Council for Interior Design Qualification

CFID–Council of Federal Interior Designers
The Governing Board for Contract Interior Design Standards

**Specialized
Associations**

ASID/NSC–American Society of Interior Designers/National
Student Council
CSID–Canadian Students of Interior Design

**Student
Associations**

All professional associations believe in advancing the
profession of interior design by

**Professional
Associations**

- serving their members
- protecting the public
- strengthening interaction between interior designers and
  industry
- strengthening interaction between interior design and the
  allied professions
- promoting design excellence
- adhering to a code of ethics
- communicating through newsletters
- educating their members through annual conferences
- supporting licensing

Apart from the obvious advantage of offering communication with other interior designers, membership in professional associations may include such benefits as

- liability insurance
- errors and omissions insurance
- continuing-education programs
- awards programs
- government and public affairs programs
- professional practice manuals, legal forms
- surveys of the profession
- group health and life insurance

In Canada, the profession is governed by provincial
legislation. IDC is an umbrella organization encompassing
the autonomous provincial associations. It was founded in
1972 by the provincial associations to provide them with a
national forum in which they could share common concerns
and experiences, find solutions to mutual problems and
create a country-wide voice for the profession.

**Associations in
Canada**

**IDC–Interior
Designers of
Canada**

Provincial associations are:
IDI–Interior Designers Institute (of British Columbia)
IDA–Interior Designers of Alberta
IDS–Interior Designers of Saskatchewan
PIDIM–Professional Interior Designers Institute of Manitoba
ARIDO–Association of Registered Interior Designers of
Ontario
SDEQ–la Société des Décorateurs-Ensembliers du Québec
IDNB–Interior Designers of New Brunswick
AIDNS–Association of Interior Designers of Nova Scotia

**Provincial
Associations**

The purpose of the Interior Designers of Canada as
listed in the Letters Patent is:

**IDC Purpose,
Goals, and
Objectives**

- to encourage excellence of interior design in the public
  interest of Canada

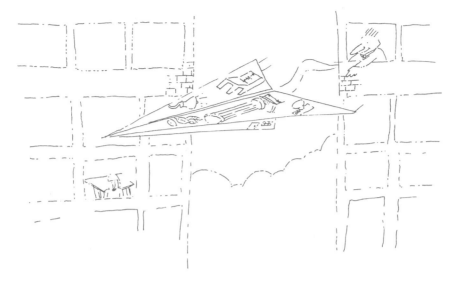

▸ to assist educational institutions in the training and development of designers
▸ to encourage the continuing education of practicing designers
▸ to assist provincial associations with research and common organizational information
▸ to uphold a code of ethics and professional practice
▸ to provide liaison between the profession and the public

The goals and objectives of the Association are:
▸ to provide opportunities for information exchange among interior design professionals
▸ to provide and promote educational programs for interior design professionals
▸ to develop and establish standards of professional knowledge and professional performance for the practice of interior design in Canada
▸ to advance the recognition and acceptance of the interior design professional by employers, other professions, governments, and the public in Canada
▸ to encourage and support research and development in the field of interior design in Canada

There is only one category of membership. It includes all those individuals who are in the highest professional category (registered or professional) in their provincial associations. For this level of membership, each provincial association requires formal education, entry-level experience, and successful completion of the NCIDQ examination. There are approximately 1700 members of IDC. IDC is a member of IFI, and liaises with IDEC, FIDER, and NCIDQ.

Associations in the United States

In the United States, professional associations are federally chartered. Most have a national office and local chapters.

ASID–American Society of Interior Designers

ASID is the world's largest association of professional interior designers. Although ASID was formed in 1975 through the consolidation of the American Institute of Interior Designers (AID) and the National Society of Interior Designers (NSID), its origins go back to 1931, with the

founding in Grand Rapids, Michigan of the American Institute
of Decorators (AID). The Society has grown into an international body with over 31,000 members. ASID embraces all the
interior design community including those specializing in
contract or residential design; working in private practice; or
employed by major corporations, design firms, or furniture
and department stores.

The purpose of the ASID is outlined in the Association's
mission statement:

"The American Society of Interior Designers is dedicated
to being the leading interior design organization and the official
source of information on all matters regarding the profession
and its practice. In so being, the Society aims to: serve its
members, protect and inform the public, advance the profession, strengthen interaction with industry and allied professions, and promote design excellence."

Membership categories are *Professional*, *Allied*, and
Student.

Professional membership recognizes an interior designer
as one who has completed a course of accredited education
and/or practical work experience in interior design or a related
field, and who has also passed the rigorous national NCIDQ
examination.

ASID is involved in many outreach and liaison activities
including membership in IFI. The association has membership
in, and/or representatives with, such organizations as the
President's Committee on Employment of the Handicapped,
the AIA Historic Preservation Committee, the National Fire
Protection Administration, and others. ASID is also involved in
lobbying and public education activities such as the homeless
issue, with both local and national involvement.

**IBD–Institute
of Business
Designers**

IBD is an organization representing professional interior
designers who specialize in commercial and institutional
design. The forerunner of IBD was conceived in 1963 by
members of the National Office Furnishings Association, and
a group was subsequently formed to provide a forum for
interior designers who were affiliated with office furnishings
dealerships. Out of this evolved IBD, formed in 1969 as an
independent organization of contract interior designers. It
has now grown to over 3500 members.

The Institute's mission statement is "Leaders together,
advancing our profession," and their goal statement is
"Through systematic methodology, attract, develop and
represent the highest calibre contract interior designer by
networking, education and advocacy."

The purpose of IBD is
- to expand the influence of contract interior designers
- to promote high ethical and design standards
- to create a better understanding of the importance and
  scope of the contract design field by the public and by professionals, thus furthering the welfare of those engaged in the
  practice of contract design
- to benefit the membership of the institute by providing an
  exchange of ideas, a common meeting group for understanding, cooperation and education, and an opportunity to keep
  abreast of developments in contract design

▸ to unite the profession, to promote the common interests of
institute members, and to advance the practice of contract
interior designers
▸ to undertake such programs and activities as may be proper
▸ to promote and enhance the welfare of the profession

There are four categories of membership: *Professional,
Affiliate, Allied,* and *Allied Organization.*

Members must have passed the NCIDQ examination and
have two years minimum experience in contract interior
design. Members are required to take advantage of continuing education opportunities.

The Institute is a member of IFI and maintains liaisons
with FIDER, NCID, AIA/IC, and the Governing Board for Contract
Interior Design Standards.

Chapters of IBD support shelters for the homeless and
various fund-raising efforts, as well as student rallies and
design competitions.

The IBD Foundation is a non-profit body sponsored by
IBD. Its broad mandate is to promote contract interior design
through community understanding and awareness.

**ISID–International
Society of
Interior Designers**

The International Society of Interior Designers, founded
in 1979 in Los Angeles by a group of nine professional
interior designers, now has a worldwide membership.

ISID supports the following goals:
▸ legal recognition of professional interior designers in order to
protect the health and welfare of the consumer and to protect against fraud and malpractice
▸ implementation of laws and studies in design to benefit the
aged, infirm, and physically impaired
▸ ongoing education for the interior designer through seminars,
lectures, and academic courses
▸ development of educational programs for students in
accredited schools of interior design, participation in appren-
ticeship programs, and placement counseling
▸ scholarships and awards
▸ participation in an exchange of international projects through
technical advice and assistance to the deprived
▸ participation in restoration and preservation of historical,
cultural, and architectural sites

- development of liaisons, coordination of mutual goals, and improvement in lines of communication with schools of environmental design
- promotion of networking, on an international level, between designers, students, industry, and related fields

There are seven membership categories: *Professional*, *Associate*, *Provisional*, *Graduate Associate*, *Student*, *Affiliate*, and *Press*.

All professional members are required to have a combination of education and experience and must have passed the NCIDQ examination. The Society maintains liaisons with IDEC, NCIDQ, and FIDER. In the community, ISID participates in charities and civic projects for the needy. ISID recognizes historical preservation of all art forms–structural, architectural, and interior–through its award program and is involved on the international and local level on several projects for restoring and preserving significant buildings.

> The term *Interior Designer* is used in most English-speaking countries; in a majority of other countries, the usual term is *Interior Architect* or its translated equivalent. Both terms are equally recognized by IFI and its member associations, and are considered to have the same meaning.

International Associations

IFI–The International Federation of Interior Architects/ Interior Designers

Founded in 1963 in Copenhagen, Denmark and now headquartered in Amsterdam, the Netherlands, IFI is comprised mainly of national interior design associations from countries around the world, in areas as far-flung as Australia, Asia, Europe, the Middle East, and North and South America. Having been founded by ten national associations representing 1400 interior architects/designers, it is now comprised of over twenty member countries including approximately 18,000 professional members and over 35,000 in other membership categories. The association maintains neutrality in respect to politics, nationality, creed, and trade unions.

Its objectives are
- to raise the standards of interior architecture/interior design and of professional practice
- to improve and expand the contribution of interior architecture/interior design to society, both in advanced and developing countries
- to initiate or further programs that are concerned with public health, safety, and welfare which apply interior architecture/ interior design to the solution of problems affecting the material and psychological well-being of man
- to serve the interests of the interior architect/interior designer, in particular, to promote the recognition of the professional designation and the professional practice
- to support the member associations where feasible

IFI promotes contact between the national associations regarding their codes of professional conduct, regulation of fee structure, and participation in competitions, and promotes the achievement of minimum standards in interior design education.
IFI also
- issues bulletins and promotes the exchange of publications
- organizes congresses, meetings, study trips, and exhibitions, and members' participation in same
- assists in the exchange of specialized teachers, speakers, trainees, and students

▸ works towards collaboration with international institutions having similar objectives
▸ actively supports, at the request of member associations, the professional interests of members within the scope of common objectives
▸ publishes a quarterly magazine, to which individuals may subscribe

IFI also collaborates with ICOGRADA (The International Council of Graphic Design Associations) and ICSID (The International Council of Societies of Industrial Design). Together the three organizations have published the *Model Code of Professional Conduct for Designers*, a set of documents regulating the conduct of international design competitions and award schemes, and the *World Directory of Schools Offering Courses in Design*. Joint congresses of these three organizations are held occasionally.

IDEC–The Interior Design Educators Council

IDEC grew out of a series of meetings held by concerned educators with a common desire to facilitate interaction between interior design educational programs. They believed that the exchange of ideas through structured conferences and networks would engender improvement and forward thinking in the education of future professional interior designers. Through their efforts IDEC was founded in 1967 and has grown to over 450 members.

The Interior Design Educators Council, Inc., is dedicated to the advancement of education and research in interior design. IDEC fosters exchange of information, improvement of educational standards, and development of the body of knowledge relative to the quality of life and human performance in the interior environment. IDEC concentrates on the establishment and strengthening of lines of communication among educators, practitioners, educational institutions, and other organizations concerned with interior design education.

IDEC was a founding member of the Foundation for Interior Design Education Research (FIDER), recognized as the official body for the accreditation of interior design programs in schools and colleges. IDEC has trustee representation on the FIDER board and its members actively participate in the accreditation process. IDEC was also a founding member of the National Council for Interior Design Qualification (NCIDQ) and has representation on the NCIDQ board.

IDEC is an international organization based in the United States.

There are eight membership categories in IDEC: *Corporate, Associate, Affiliate, Graduate, Liaison, Emeritus, Honorary*, and *Fellow*.

Corporate members have diplomas or degrees in interior design or a related field from an accredited school, college, or university, and a minimum of two years of experience as a full-time interior design education in a department offering a program in interior design.

IDEC maintains liaison with FIDER, NCIDQ, IFI, ASID, IBD, IDC, ISID, AIA/IC (American Institute of Architects/Interiors Committee), IALD (International Association of Lighting Designers), IES (Illuminating Engineering Society), IFMA (International Facilities Management Association), and BIFMA (Business-Institutional Furniture Manufacturers Association).

Special benefits of membership in IDEC include:
- ▸ IDEC *Comprehensive Bibliography for Interior Designers*, the only bibliography specific to interior design, published biannually
- ▸ placement opportunities
- ▸ position paper on criteria for evaluation of interior design faculty for tenure and promotion
- ▸ career guidance
- ▸ continuing education opportunities
- ▸ networking
- ▸ annual conference
- ▸ quarterly newsletter *Record*
- ▸ *Journal of Interior Design Education Research*; IDEC publishes *JIDER* twice yearly. It is the only juried journal on interior design.

**Credential-
Granting
Associations**

The training (education and early professional practice) of interior designers is regulated and controlled by a number of national and international associations. In this regard the profession is not unlike others such as architecture, law, engineering, or medicine. All of these professions are self-regulating and have a common purpose, to assure a high degree of capability and expertise to those who use these professional services.

Interior designers should be familiar with credential-granting associations and their purposes—accrediting interior design programs and qualifying practitioners. Many regional associations have enacted licensing legislation that clearly stipulates who may practice under the designation *professional* and what services they may perform.

**FIDER—The
Foundation for
Interior Design
Education
Research**

FIDER, an international agency, was formed by the signing of an Indenture of Trust in 1970, and first met formally in 1971. The signators were representatives of the American Institute of Interior Design, (AID), the National Society of Interior Designers, (NSID), and IDEC. FIDER is the organization that accredits interior design programs in institutions of higher learning in the United States and Canada. The primary purpose of the accreditation process is to ensure a consistently high level of quality of education. A Board of Trustees, which governs the foundation, is composed of representatives of ASID, IDEC, IBD, and IDC.

**The FIDER Trust
Purpose
Statement**

The FIDER Trust's purpose is stated:

"This Trust is created and shall be operated for the purpose of establishing and administering a voluntary plan for the special accreditation of programs of interior design education offered at institutions of higher learning located throughout the United States, its possessions and Canada. Such plan shall emphasize the use of accreditation procedures to assure that the purposes and accomplishments of programs of interior design education meet the needs of society, interior design students and the interior design profession, and serve as a means of protecting the public against professional incompetence."

In order to carry out its stated purpose, the Trust shall:
- ▸ promote and support research and investigation necessary to establish criteria for the evaluation of programs of interior design education in institutions of higher education

▸ establish criteria in the areas of curriculum, faculty, administration and physical facilities to be used as a basis for voluntary accreditation of programs of interior design education
▸ structure the ways and means for voluntary accreditation of
  interior design programs under accepted national standards
  for accreditation, and conduct such activity as may be necessary to assure eventual recognition of the Trust's accreditation plan by the National Commission on Accrediting
▸ encourage all institutions of higher education offering programs in interior design to voluntarily participate in the
  accreditation program, and offer counsel to those institutions seeking to improve their programs of study
▸ establish a program of continuing research and investigation
  to assure that accreditation criteria continue to reflect current practices in education and professional interior design

Accreditation procedures assure that the purposes and
accomplishments of programs of interior design education
meet the needs of interior design students, the profession,
and society.

The voluntary accreditation process reviews programs
using internationally recognized educational standards. An
on-site visit and peer evaluation is made by a team composed of practitioners and educators. Recommendations are
sent to the Board of Trustees for final accreditation action. If
accreditation standards have been met, accreditation is
granted to the program for three or six years.

**Three Levels of
Accreditation**

Accreditation at the **Pre-professional Assistant Level** of
education is directed toward those programs that, typically
through a two-year time frame, prepare the students for
positions as design assistants, merchandisers, delineators,
estimators, and so on. This education is generally considered
a terminal level that does not normally lead to practice as a
professional interior designer. However, individual institutions
may grant some credits from these programs toward the
achievement of the First Professional Degree Level.

Accreditation at the **First Professional Degree Level** of
education is directed toward those programs that provide
academic preparation for the professional interior designer.
This preparation is the first component of a sequence that
includes formal education, entry-level experience, and
satisfactory completion of a qualifying examination.

Accreditation at the **Post-professional Master's Degree**
level of education is directed towards those programs which
provide an individual the opportunity to engage in research or
creative design work within the context of interior design, and
this activity culminates in a graphic or written thesis. The
common body of knowledge as contained in a First Professional Degree Level interior design program is a prerequisite.

FIDER's policies and procedures regarding the accreditation process have been developed in conformance with the
guidelines and directives of the Council on Post-Secondary
Accreditation and the U.S. Department of Education, and are
subject to their review and approval. Any post-secondary
interior design program in the U.S. or Canada may apply for
accreditation by FIDER, regardless of the school or department under which it is administered.

FIDER has an active research committee that validates the accreditation process through studies, identifies interior design programs, and encourages research in interior design. Also, a standards committee composed of educators and practitioners monitors the standards with periodic surveys and revisions, in concert with direction from the educational institutions and the profession. Lists of accredited programs are published, along with their current accreditation status and next scheduled review.

FIDER's work is accomplished by volunteers who are assisted by a small professional staff. It is supported by charitable contributions and accreditation review fees. FIDER is recognized by the design profession internationally as the leading organization in determining the hallmarks of a quality education in interior design.

NCIDQ is an independent organization created in the public interest to establish standards for the qualification of professional interior designers. The Council has been in existence since 1972 and was incorporated in 1974.

NCIDQ–National Council for Interior Design Qualification

The stated purpose of NCIDQ is:

The NCIDQ Statement of Purpose

"To contribute to the public acceptance and professional and legal recognition of the interior design practitioner through

▸ administering a valid and reliable minimum competency examination
▸ administrative and data support to facilitate legal recognition
▸ promotional efforts to increase public awareness of the profession and its concern for public health, safety, and welfare
▸ guidelines for codes of conduct and recommended practices
▸ recertification."

The NCIDQ Council identifies those interior designers who have met the minimum standards for professional practice. It endeavors to maintain the most advanced examining procedures and to constantly revise its examination to reflect expanding professional knowledge and design-development techniques. NCIDQ seeks the acceptance of its examination as a universal standard by which to measure the competency of interior designers to practice as professionals. The NCIDQ examination is a prerequisite for professional membership in participating design associations. It must also be passed in order to obtain a license to practice interior design or to be registered as an interior designer in those states of the U.S.A. and provinces in Canada that have licensing or registration statutes governing the profession.

Examinations are held at testing centers in the U.S. and Canada in mid-April and mid-October. The present examination is the product of many years of research and development by qualified professional interior designers and interior design educators, and a professional testing agency.

The examination is updated periodically to reflect the realities of current practice. Jurying and grading procedures are adjusted to reflect the latest developments and to maintain the greatest possible degree of fairness.

Membership is organizational, not individual. Members are ASID, IBD, ISP, IDC, IDEC, ISID, those states with licensing boards, and provincial professional associations with licensing responsibilities.

NCIDQ maintains that through standard and consistent use of the NCIDQ exam, reciprocal registration of interior designers throughout the states and provinces may be facilitated.

A research committee focuses on job analysis, candidates' profiles, statistics development and assessment, legislative evaluation, definition development, and examination development.

**Strategic Goals
of NCIDQ**

NCIDQ's strategic goals are

▶ to formulate and administer a legally and statistically defensible examination which is recognized as the basis for minimum competency of the interior design profession

▶ to identify and implement services which will contribute to the qualification and recognition of practitioners

▶ to provide assistance to international design organizations, state/provincial boards, and individual professionals seeking legal recognition

▶ to interact with member organizations, state and provincial bodies, and other related professions through open communication and coordination of programs and services

▶ to inform the public-at-large of the unique body of knowledge and the professional qualifications of NCIDQ–certified interior design practitioners

▶ to accomplish its strategic goals and fulfill its mission through effective management practices and financial autonomy

NCIDQ has an executive administrator and office staff. It also avails itself of the expertise of advisors, lawyers, statisticians, design-problem authors, and question writers.

**Specialized
Associations**

**CFID–Council of
Federal Interior
Designers**

The Council of Federal Interior Designers (CFID), incorporated in 1986, is an organization of professionals employed by the U.S. federal government in interior design and space-planning programs.

The purpose of this organization is communication and exchange of information in order to promote design excellence in government interiors and professionalism in federal design programs.

**Governing Board
for Contract
Interior Design
Standards**

The Governing Board is a creation of the Institute of Business Designers (IBD) and was founded in 1987. It is composed of six certified contract interior designers.

The purpose of the Governing Board is to promote the professional competence of contract interior designers and to enhance the prestige of the profession through the improvement of its public image.

The Board's goals and objectives are

▶ to elevate the status of the contract interior design profession through greater end-user awareness and knowledge of the scope of services offered by the competent contract interior designer

▶ to provide the Certified Contract Interior Designer with benefits by continually validating the process and competencies to assure proper positioning and program excellence

▶ to ensure that employers can identify qualified practitioners by certification status

- to provide a career guide and path of self-development for contract interior designers, students, and educators including continuing education and commitment to the profession
- to influence the evolution of the profession of contract interior design through research and education

Certification

- measures self-improvement, continued learning and service to the profession
- assists in advancement of personal prestige
- provides a vehicle for peer and industry recognition
- creates marketing advantages

Requirements for certification include education and testing, six years of continuous contract interior design experience and, if required by the state or province of practice, a license. Recertification is required every three years.

Student Associations

In interior design, as in many professions, there is a gap between academic training and actual practice. Interior design student associations, and student memberships in professional associations, narrow the gap as much as possible through student-to-student and student-to-professional interaction.

Through memberships, students are introduced to the professional aspects of an interior design career. Classroom activities take on additional meaning when students interact with professionals and become aware of facets of interior design that cannot be covered within academic programs.

Value of Student Association Memberships

Participation in student associations
- helps prepare the student for the future, and thereby contributes to the profession
- promotes contacts with manufacturers and their representatives
- allows the student to contribute to the quality of interior design education
- assists in projecting an accurate image and developing awareness of interior design within academic institutions, college communities, and the public at large

The American Society of Interior Designers (ASID) has a student membership category and student chapters. An annual meeting, the National Student Connection, is held concurrently with the ASID Annual Conference.

The International Society of Interior Designers (ISID) also has a student membership category. It invites students to its annual conferences, holds chapter meetings, and conducts an annual scholarship/competition.

In Canada, work was begun on a national student association–Canadian Students of Interior Design (CSID)–in 1987 and officially endorsed in 1989.

Summary

All of these North American associations connected with the field of interior design have been working in concert for the past several years to help the profession take its rightful place in the family of professions that deal with human habitation and the built environment. Recent areas of involvement have been accreditation, testing, licensing, and monitored internship for entry-level professionals. Through meetings of leaders and joint task forces, the multifaceted profession becomes focused on common issues for the benefit of mankind.

Licensing

Interior designers are part of the whole spectrum of specialists–architects, engineers, contractors, laborers, sub-trades, and others–who work together to create the built environment. They are a link in the chain of responsibility; however, generally speaking, there is no governmental assurance of the qualifications of practitioners. Licensing is the vehicle which provides protection for the general public.

Interior design is a profession and a business in which laws and codes of business practice prevail. A good licensing act gives teeth to ethical and moral considerations.

By definition, interior designers work "...in order to enhance the quality of life and protect the health, safety, and welfare of the public." Services concerned with the health, safety, and welfare of the public that fall into the daily work of interior designers are: space planning; furniture planning; interior construction and detailing; lighting; heating, ventilation, and air-conditioning; site inspection; building and fire regulations; drawings and specifications; project management. Working in these areas obligates interior designers to act in a fully professional manner and accept the liabilities inherent in that action.

Interior designers are members of teams of professionals jointly involved in the construction, furnishing, and equipping of the built environment for the use of the general public. As team members, liability exists in conjunction with the other disciplines, as well as in those areas which fall completely within the purview of the interior designer.

Just as engineers, architects, and the building trades are licensed in order to assure the public a standard of qualification, so too should the interior designer be licensed. Assuring qualifications for performing work professionally is the main reason for licensing, which in turn protects the welfare of the public. This has been recognized in many states and throughout most of Canada.

Licensing acts are a state or provincial (or other jurisdictional area) prerogative and must be enacted at that level. The initiative for seeking legislation must come from a local organization or other legally constituted group. The rationale for licensing addresses three main concerns: that interior designers have separate and distinct expertise that is different from other professionals; that this expertise contributes to public health, safety, and welfare; and that persons using such professionals' services be assured of their qualifications.

Licensing Acts

There are two basic forms of licensing acts: a *Practice Act* and a *Title Act*. In some legislative jurisdictions one type of act is required; in others either type may be put forward.

A title act protects the use of the title *interior designer* (sometimes in conjunction with the word *professional, registered*, or *certified),* and gives assurance to the public that anyone using the title has the professional qualifications to do so.

A title act may state: "No one not licensed under this Act may use the title *interior designer* but may perform the same type of services under a different title, such as architect, interior decorator, space designer."

A practice act restricts the practice of interior design to individuals licensed under the act.

A practice act may state: "No one not licensed under this Act may practice the profession of interior design nor use the title *interior designer*." A separate clause usually excludes architects from the practice provisions of the Act.

In either case, architects should be exempt from any restriction on practicing interior design.

Professional interior designers are accorded a significant level of trust–personal, financial, and otherwise–by clients, the general public, and members of other professions. It is imperative that this trust be backed by competence and, of course, honesty, integrity, and objectivity.

To provide models of conduct for interior designers who deal with complex personal/business relationships, various codes of ethics have been formulated. These codes combine business practices with moral principles, enabling designers to uphold this trust in the practice of their profession.

Codes of ethical behavior exist within the professional organizations described in this chapter. Included in the appendix are the Codes of Ethics from ASID, IBD, IDC, and IFI.

The concept of professional ethics is apparent in such enforceable rules, regulations, and prohibitions, but usually these are minimum standards of acceptable behavior. It is in the best interest of the profession to strive for unswerving commitment to honorable conduct. Professional designers should always maintain integrity and objectivity. They should observe the profession's highest standards and strive to continually improve their competence and the quality of service.

Licensing acts describe ethical conduct under headings such as disclosure, relations with clients, and responsibilities to clients, colleagues, and others.

Professional Ethics

This area of ethical conduct deals with the self-representation of designers, or what is disclosed or not disclosed to clients and the public.

Disclosure: Conduct and Practices

A list of disclosure items may include
- refraining from making misleading, deceptive, or false statements or claims regarding professional qualifications, experience, abilities, or performance
- conforming to all existing laws, regulations, and business procedures as established by the government in the locale of practice
- clearly identifying, using names and/or stamps, any work done for a client (the use of names and/or stamps on any work that is not the designer's, or that has not been carried out under the designer's direction and supervision, is not permitted)
- ensuring that the interior design services are clearly identified when listing credits for projects

If professionals are licensed, then the following legally enforceable rules regarding professional relations with clients will be in place.

Designer-Client Relationships

If unlicensed, professional designers are morally bound by the same regulations, as follows:

▶ to ensure that any interior design services provided to a client conform with all applicable laws and regulations
▶ to disclose to clients any financial interests that the designers may have in a project or in the provision of goods or services to any project
▶ to refrain from requesting or accepting any fee, commission, reward, advantage, or benefit of any kind from suppliers of goods and/or services in return for specifying and/or purchasing such material for a client
▶ to respect the confidentiality of any information derived from a client
▶ to refrain from advertising professional services in a manner which may bring the practice of interior design into disrepute

Responsibilities to Clients

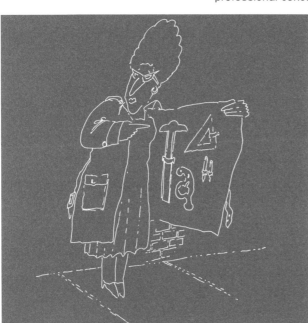

Interior designers should be fair and candid with their clients and serve them to the best of their abilities with professional concern for the clients' best interests, and consistent with their responsibilities to the public.

Before undertaking any project, designers and their clients should determine the scope of the work, the nature and extent of the services to be performed, and the fees. Written confirmation of these details should follow. In performing design services, communication with the client should be maintained regarding the project, its potential solutions, and its estimated probable costs. Designers should guard the interests of their clients and the rights of those whose contracts they administer.

When representing clients, the best possible contractual arrangements should be made with contractors, manufacturers, and suppliers. It is also professionally important to maintain fair and responsible dealings with these other businesses.

Responsibilities to Colleagues

Professional designers should conduct themselves in a manner that promotes cooperation and good relations within the profession. They should contribute to the interchange of technical information and experience between interior design and the allied professions, and respect the interests and contributions of other professionals.

Designers may find themselves called upon to comment on other interior designers' work and, in a consultative capacity, may reasonably be expected to do so. While personal opinion may play a significant part in a critique, the fine line between objective and subjective criticism should be maintained. Personal denigration should be avoided.

Other Responsibilities

The public is generally unaware of the qualifications required of professional interior designers. In order to enhance the stature of the profession and its ability to serve the public, designers should be aware of their own professional conduct and act ethically and responsibly.

The following are some of the guidelines:

- Competition is part of any profession; however, designers should maintain their professionalism when competing against other designers.
- Designers should not undertake any work that they cannot reasonably expect to complete with professional competence.
- In the performance of professional services, designers should not allow their own financial or other interests to affect the exercise of independent professional judgment on behalf of their clients.
- Should designers become involved in projects that seem unsafe or economically unfeasible, or about which they have serious legal reservations, the clients should be given written notification of the designers' concerns.
- Accepting gifts or other benefits may place designers in positions of unprofessional obligation to the donors. It is best to avoid such obligations.

Career Opportunities

The public's demand for interior design services has grown rapidly, especially in the last decade. With that growth has come a wider range of specialties in the field.

Types of Projects

Today designers may choose to specialize in residential design of houses, apartments, and condominiums, or in diverse areas of non-residential contract design.

Interior designers are involved in design for
- offices and other work settings
- the hospitality industry: restaurants, hotels, resorts
- health-related facilities: hospitals, clinics, senior citizens' care homes
- retail: department stores, chain stores, specialty shops
- places of worship
- educational facilities and libraries
- entertainment facilities
- museums
- government facilities, from post offices to submarines
- transportation: terminals, trains, ships, airplanes, spacecraft

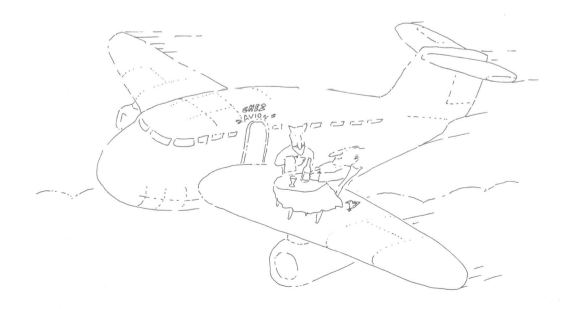

Interior designers may also specialize in set design for stage/screen productions, lighting design, color consultation, product development, marketing research, teaching, journalism, illustration, programming, space planning, facility planning, or historic preservation.

Career Options

Interior designers find professional employment in diverse settings:
- interior design firms
- office furnishings dealers with interior design departments
- retail establishments with interior design departments
- in-house departments within
    corporations
    institutions
    government agencies
    medical/health-care facilities
    hotels, motels
    restaurant/hospitality industries
    builders, developers, contractors
- architectural firms
- research
- historic restoration specialists
- educators in post-secondary institutions

Most interior design firms deal with a variety of projects—from residential design to restaurants to ceremonial spaces. Within the vast array of project areas, some firms may specialize in, for instance, working spaces, or educational facilities, or culture and leisure spaces, or hospitality (restaurants, hotels, and so on) or health-care facilities, or a combination of several. Within these specialties some projects will focus on such aspects as space planning, others on detailing of built-in furniture.

Types of Positions

Interior designers hold a variety of positions and levels of employment such as
- principal of a firm
- director of a department
- senior manager
- senior designer
- junior designer
- self-employed designer

The incomes of interior designers vary depending upon location, volume of business, experience, and professional reputation.

Employment in Education

Higher visibility and expanded options in the profession mean that more young people, and mature individuals seeking a career change, want to study interior design. Therefore there is a need for interior design educators.

For employment as an educator, most institutions require the common body of knowledge of interior design plus a post-professional master's degree.

Experience in the field is advisable before entering a graduate program with a view to concentrating on teaching. Passing of the NCIDQ exam is also recommended. The combination of graduate-level education and experience is also the basis for research and creative design work, and it should be noted that most educators maintain a practice or conduct research as well as teach.

Occupational Variables

When choosing employment, designers should consider these important aspects, which provide wide choice within the occupation:

Types of Projects
- ► contract
- ► residential
- ► institutional
- ► hospitality
- ► transportation

In each of these areas, projects may be large or small and the design firm may specialize or may offer a mix of design services.

Scope of Work
- ► complete project
- ► partial project (such as detailing only)
- ► working drawings
- ► specifications
- ► perspectives
- ► programming

Working Environment
- ► department: team or individual
- ► size of office
- ► resources available, such as samples, supplies, printing/duplicating, CADD (computer assisted drafting and design)
- ► consultants available
- ► autonomy of the interior design department
- ► opportunities for advancement

Responsibility
- ► degree of personal responsibility
- ► to user
- ► to client
- ► to employer

Contacts
- ► suppliers
- ► consultants
- ► the public
- ► government authorities
- ► regulatory agencies

Remuneration
- ► fixed salary
- ► profit sharing
- ► overtime
- ► benefits, such as group insurance: life, health, dental

Advantages
- ► interaction with fellow employees
- ► valuable experience
- ► personally rewarding work
- ► encouragement of creativity/innovation
- ► travel opportunities

Interior Design Business Management

II

Business Basics

Business is business. The principles of business organization and management are the same regardless of the product or service being offered. The interior design business is a professional service much like law, dentistry, or architecture. All designers should be familiar with the basics of business outlined in this chapter.

Organization

Businesses are formed to meet perceived needs in the community and require proper "market assessment" to increase the likelihood of long-term viability. A market assessment is a composite of observation, research, and deductive thinking. Areas to assess are the competition, the demand for interior design services, the economy, the locale, and the particular service being offered.

Having made realistic assessments and decided upon a particular focus and market, the design firm would organize for business by taking the following steps:

Steps in Forming a Business

▸ 1. Determine the type of practice and set up the business with advice from a lawyer and an accountant.
▸ 2. Arrange financing.
▸ 3. Secure appropriate insurance coverage.
▸ 4. Develop a management system and all the proper forms for conducting business.
▸ 5. Investigate and decide on probable fee structures and contracts.
▸ 6. Plan and implement an effective marketing program.

This section deals with the basics of the first four steps; the last two are such vital components of any business that they are outlined separately.

Designers contemplating business ownership should first assess their ability to be in business. Refer to publications that outline the pros and cons of being an entrepreneur or independent business owner. In addition to design expertise, many other characteristics and strengths are needed to run a business, whether alone or in partnership. Designers should have confidence in their design ability, trust their own technical competence, have some experience as organizers, and be able to work well with others. The various types of interior design businesses may then be considered.

Types of Business

Because laws and regulations differ from area to area, lawyers and accountants are essential for advice regarding concerns within the specific locale. A business may be organized as a *Sole Proprietorship, Partnership, Limited Partnership, Corporation, Cooperative,* or *Subchapter S.*

Sole Proprietorship

This is the simplest and least expensive type of business. The company and the individual owner are the same. The proprietor is both controlling manager and owner of all the company's assets, receives all profits, and is personally responsible for all losses. Organization does not require substantial legal formalities, but simply the following:

▸ deciding upon the name and location of the firm
▸ registering the name with the appropriate authority
▸ registering with the required tax offices
▸ opening a bank account in the firm's name
▸ establishing credit and trade sources
▸ printing business cards, stationery, and appropriate forms

Personal Traits Best Suited to Entrepreneurship

▸ ambition
▸ motivation
▸ maturity
▸ self-discipline
▸ self-confidence
▸ willingness to take risks
▸ responsibility
▸ decisiveness
▸ honesty
▸ persistence
▸ assertiveness
▸ innovation
▸ friendliness
▸ attentiveness
▸ persuasiveness
▸ energy
▸ health
▸ resistance to stress

With this type of business, the designer/owner should be aware of the possible dangers inherent in unlimited liability and potential income tax disadvantages.

As stated, the individual owner is liable for all losses. The designer/owner is also responsible for all start-up costs, all debts, and any other results of the operation. These responsibilities are in no way limited, except those which may be covered by insurance. Creditors are legally within their rights to take action against the owner's personal assets if their bills are not paid by the company. (See "Professional Liability," page 35.)

Tax implications are similar. Profits from the business are regarded as net income for the designer and must be declared on personal tax returns. There are few, if any, tax concessions for a sole proprietor. Rules regarding income tax vary, and sole proprietors must be prepared to outline their personal financial situation, including other income, spouse's income, and debts, to a chartered accountant in the locale of practice.

A sole proprietorship may not use "Incorporated," "Limited," or "Corporation" as part of its name, but may use the word "Company." The business name may be the individual's own name (perhaps with "Company," "Interiors," or "Interior Design") or any created name. A created name must first be checked with the appropriate authority, on the advice of a lawyer, and registered.

Partnership

A partnership consists of two or more individuals and may be established on any basis other than as a corporation. It is an efficient way of apportioning risks, work-load, and profits or losses. Responsibilities are shared and the talents and experiences of each partner can complement and reinforce the whole. A partnership is easy to enter into, but should not be undertaken lightly.

Generally, legal jurisdictions have some form of partnership act in force as a basis for settling disputes. A lawyer, or the appropriate department of government, is the source for such a document, and it is advisable that it be obtained and studied.

Details Covered by a Partnership Act

An act will define such details as:
▸ A partnership is a form of commercial association, other than a corporation, organized with a view to profit.
▸ A general partnership is one in which members are individually, and with other partners jointly and severally, liable for all debts and obligations incurred in the name of the firm.
▸ A partnership must be dissolved and reconstituted if/when a partner leaves, retires, or dies, or when there is an unresolved dispute.
▸ Outgoing partners are liable for debts incurred before leaving unless released by other partners *and* creditors.
▸ Incoming partners are not liable for debts incurred before entry into the partnership.

- Each partner's share of the profits from business income is considered personal income for taxation purposes.
- The actions (such as commitments, promises, losses, mistakes, damages, lapses) of any one partner are the responsibility of, and binding upon, all partners.

A Formal Agreement of Partnership

A partnership should not be entered into without a formal agreement. Legal counsel should be sought after the potential partners have outlined details such as

- the capital contribution of each partner
- any contributions *in kind*, such as furnishings, equipment, office space, clients
- payment schedule for costs incurred when not adequately covered by capital
- description of responsibilities
- work load
- use of draw accounts
- schedule of operating expenses
- banking arrangements, including signing authority
- share structure for profits
- method of dissolution, whether by unilateral decision, mutual agreement, retirement, or death

A partnership should only be contemplated when the individuals feel they know and understand each other, know that their personalities are compatible, and know that each will carry a fair share of the work load. Sometimes the discussions preceding the outline of agreement reveal more about the partners than was previously known. It is advisable that any possible areas of disagreement be disclosed in advance. For a successful partnership, it is essential that each partner be assured of an equitable division of labor and responsibility.

The greatest disadvantage to the partnership type of practice is the aspect of unlimited liability. Individual partners will be personally liable for all financial losses or claims upon the partnership. Business errors, misjudgements, irresponsibility, or the bad luck of any one partner must be covered by the personal resources of the remaining partner(s).

It is not possible to accumulate capital in a partnership. Income in excess of business expenditures is regarded as personal income shared by the partners. An accountant in the locale of practice should be consulted for specific tax regulations.

Limited Partnership

A limited partnership must have at least one general partner, who assumes all liability for business losses. In limited partnerships, one or more partners may have limited or no liability. Limited partners may be silent partners who invest in the business but have restricted input–or no say at all–in the operation. Such a partner trusts the acumen and ability of the active partner(s) to make a profit in which he or she then shares. In the case of business failure, limited partners lose their investments but their personal assets cannot be touched by creditors.

Incorporation

Unlike proprietorship or partnership, a limited company or corporation is a legal entity.

The corporate title may be (Name) Company Limited, (Name) Corporation, (Name) Corporation Limited, or (Name) Incorporated, or their abbreviated forms.

Setting up a corporation requires an initial outlay for legal and government fees. Accounting and reporting procedures are involved and generally require the services of professional accountants. A firm may be incorporated in a state, a province, or a nation. Federal incorporation is most costly; it is necessary when the business will be operating outside of the home jurisdiction. Shareholders may increase or decrease in number and in amount of investment. Shares may be sold without disrupting the corporate entity.

The firm may be incorporated to provide interior design services only, or it may be a design firm which includes architecture, landscape architecture, graphic design, and/or industrial design, as well as interior design.

Advantages of Incorporation

The main advantages of incorporation are the limitations on liability and the tax benefit (tax on profits is less than that levied on personal income).

Limited liability is the most important advantage: business debts are the corporation's responsibility. The owner (or owners) are shareholders, with no personal liability for debts incurred by the company. (In some jurisdictions, directors have a degree of liability–for unpaid wages, for instance–and it is essential to ascertain the legal requirements in the locale of practice.)

In order to operate a business on borrowed capital or to maintain a line of credit, financial institutions will generally require the principal owner(s) or investor(s) to personally guarantee the obligation. This effectively negates the advantage of limited liability on the part of the shareholders, so far as the debt to the financial institution is concerned. Other debts to creditors will, of course, remain the sole responsibility of the corporation.

A corporation must be used responsibly. The advantage of limited liability can be nullified if designers order materials or maintain practices in their own names. *All* business must be conducted in the name of the corporation; it is the umbrella which protects designers from the considerable risks involved in the practice of interior design.

Corporate tax is generally in the range of 20 to 25 percent of earnings (profit), which is significantly lower than income tax payable on personal income. It is possible to accumulate profits in a corporation, which can then be used for business development or for salaries, if and when business income is reduced.

There are other benefits for individual owner(s) of a corporation. A qualified accountant can outline and clarify them.

Benefits of Corporate Ownership

The following points may be raised:
- pension benefits
- medical/dental group insurance plans
- profit sharing
- transfer of investments to the corporation
- payments of "salary" to family members, which lessens individual income tax
- deferred dividends
- restrictions that apply if principals change

There are also disadvantages to incorporation, especially the necessity to keep all records in scrupulous order and to report on corporate affairs to appropriate government bodies. While legal requirements are stringent, they are certainly manageable if the firm obtains appropriate legal and financial advice at the outset. In addition, the costs of incorporation are much higher than for setting up a sole proprietorship or partnership.

In summary, a corporation is a stable, entirely business-like way of conducting an interior design practice. With certain clients, particularly other corporations, incorporation makes its own statement about the designers' professionalism.

The Cooperative

A cooperative is a distinct form of corporate entity, formed and operated to provide its shareholders with goods or services. Capital invested by the members is limited by legislation; each shareholder, regardless of the number of shares held, has one vote. Surplus income is returned to the shareholders as dividends, proportionate to the business done by the individual shareholder with or through the cooperative.

Subchapter S (U.S.A.)

The Subchapter S type of corporation is permitted to operate as a corporate entity, with one difference: it is taxed as a partnership rather than as a corporation. It is allowed to forego payment of corporate taxes, but must be registered with the Internal Revenue Service (IRS) prior to incorporation. Profits are distributed to the owners as capital gains; losses are assumed by the shareholders, and are reported on their personal tax returns.

This innovative type of corporation and tax structure is subject to change; legal and financial advice should be sought regarding local tax regulations for Subchapter S.

Professional Counsel

It is essential that all designers understand the challenge of business and its potential rewards. For anyone in business, successful operation is based on recognizing deficiencies in business acumen, then locating, consulting with, and following the advice of professionals who have the needed expertise and experience. As well, professional associations and government departments often publish information helpful to business people.

Interior design firms consult professionals in the following four areas: accounting, law, insurance, and banking. The following is a brief description of each service.

Accounting and Accountants

Because money–the universal medium of exchange between people, goods, and services–is involved in virtually all business transactions, solid advice on the handling and recording of funds is of prime importance. The accountant's expertise is in relating other business functions to *the bottom line*–the eventual profit or loss. As government is involved in every business, both as a regulator and a tax receiver, financial records must be structured so that they are standardized and accessible for audit at any time.

Accountants assist in the set-up of a firm's bookkeeping system, which is designed to record and control the flow of financial information. They may also register a new company with the appropriate taxation authorities and other regulatory agencies. Tax laws are peculiar to the locale of practice;

besides tax on income or profit, there may be sales tax, payroll tax, business tax, tax deductions to be collected from employees and remitted to the government. There are also tax exemptions, forward averaging, amortization of capital costs, and so on, which the accountant will review, and which will impact on the eventual success of the firm.

Large firms may employ an accountant who tracks the company finances and manages the books on a daily basis. Annual statements are then sent to a secondary accounting firm for a yearly audit.

Small firms find individuals within their limited staff (principals and employees) to do the daily bookkeeping, to maintain the records, to participate in financial planning, and to prepare all documents for the annual financial review by the firm's accountant.

Financial statements may be *audited*—each transaction personally checked by the accounting firm—or *unaudited*, in which case the accountant writes a disclaimer saying that the statements have been prepared from the client's records only. Audited statements are more costly and are generally not required unless there is suspicion of tax evasion or other illegality.

Legal Counsel

Every business must be set up according to the law in the locale of practice and registered with the appropriate government agencies. These duties are undertaken by a firm's lawyer, who also advises on such matters as the signing of leases for premises or equipment, zoning restrictions for business occupancy, legal dealings with staff and financial institutions, areas of professional liability, and possible business casualties that must be covered by insurance.

Lawyers may also be asked for their opinion on any proposed contracts, whether with clients or with suppliers, contractors, or others.

Insurance

Basic insurance for a business covers loss of premises and contents by fire, theft, vandalism, or other calamity. The same policy also protects business owners from claims for personal injury suffered by staff and others while on the premises.

Partnership insurance is available for those sharing in the expenses and income of a business, and there is also insurance coverage for individuals who are off work for extended periods due to illness. Liability insurance is a necessity. Designers' liabilities are considerable. (This subject is fully covered below.) Contracts for insurance should be checked by a lawyer for appropriateness.

Banking

A commercial bank account with a hefty balance is trouble-free. It is also most unusual. Most businesses operate to some degree on credit.

A *line of credit* gives a firm the ability to overdraw the account up to a specific amount. Overdrafts are considered short-term loans, and the principal(s) of the firm will have to sign promissory notes in advance so that, as funds are needed by the firm, money can be put into the account. As soon as there are deposits to the account, the loaned amounts are withdrawn by the bank. While the bank's money is in the firm's use, interest is charged.

A bank requires business collateral, such as accounts receivable, or a personal guarantee backed by some form of collateral, or a combination, in order to set the limit for the line of credit. For a new business, the value of collateral required is approximately four times the requested maximum loan. For a $25,000 line of credit, $100,000 in collateral or guarantee will be necessary. If a line of credit is granted, the bank will probably request that it be named the beneficiary on the business insurance policy.

A bank will also wish to be kept informed, on a monthly basis, of accounts receivable. The manager (or loans officer) will be particularly interested in the financial prospects of the business and will want to see a statement of the anticipated cash flow.

A financial institution is important, not only for its lending capacity, but because it is the prime credit reference for a business. As well, banks may advise on the suitability of listing with established credit-rating agencies.

> ▸ *collateral:* stocks, bonds, or other possessions pledged as security for a loan
> ▸ *accounts receivable:* a record of sales made for which money is still owing
> ▸ *cash flow:* the volume of cash received and/or paid out in a given period

Professional Liability

When an interior designer or firm enters into a contract and specifies interior finishes, furnishings, or equipment, the individual or entity becomes liable for the performance of the goods specified. While this has always been the case, licensing of interior designers has drawn attention to the situation. It is anticipated that liability suits will begin to increase–as they have for architects and engineers.

Professional negligence could arise from a designer's failure to condemn defective work. Liability could also stem from the designer's failure to specify the correct construction system, material, or furniture for the particular use.

In signing a contract to perform design work, the designer implies professional competence and therefore can be sued for producing below-standard work. Compliance with building and fire codes is also imperative, and failure to comply could be considered professional negligence.

Purchase and resale of furniture, furnishings, and equipment places the designer in the *chain of distribution* and therefore liable under both implied and specific product warranties. ASID advises its members to refrain from purchasing other than as an agent of the owner/client.

An owner/client's loss of income due to delay in the completion of a project, particularly if caused by an error on the part of the designer, leaves the designer open to a claim for losses.

If injury or damage occurs as a direct result of the designer's drawings, design, or specifications, the designer will be held responsible.

Two frequent sources of claims are inaccurate measurements and specification of furniture unsuitable for the intended use.

Lawsuits Are Avoidable

There are several simple actions that a designer may take to lessen the possibility of being sued:

- ▶ Have liability insurance and errors and omissions insurance. These kinds of insurance may be taken out separately on each project. Consider passing the cost along to the client.
- ▶ Retain consultants for those areas of a project which are outside the expertise of an interior designer, such as structural, mechanical, electrical engineering; landscaping; and so on.
- ▶ Sign contracts with the client that spell out the precise areas of responsibility and services to be performed. Use clear language.
- ▶ Comply with the building and fire codes applicable to the project. Ignorance of the code is no defence.
- ▶ Use known and reliable contractors, sub-contractors, workrooms, and so on.
- ▶ Keep accurate and up-to-date records of the project. Proper documentation may be the best defence.
- ▶ Consult a lawyer.

Professional liability insurance protects the insured party against liability for damages arising out of the insured's performance of professional services as an interior designer. It should also cover the cost of investigation and defense of any claims during the term of the policy.

**Professional
Liability
Insurance**

Professional liability insurance has advantages for both interior designers and their clients. The biggest benefit to the designer is the insurance company's obligation to defend all claims against the designer during the term of the policy, even if such claims prove to be groundless or fraudulent. In many cases, this obligation can be more valuable than the agreement to pay a claim for which the insured is found liable. The investigation and defense of claims can be very expensive. Costs of investigators, experts, and lawyers may exceed the amount of the claim itself.

A further advantage is the protection afforded against the errors or omissions of other partners or employees of a firm. Designers may be willing to risk the consequences of their own mistakes, but hesitate to expose themselves to liability from the mistakes of others. Employees also benefit knowing they are protected in the event of a claim arising out of a mistake on their part.

Having professional liability insurance conveys a fiscally responsible position. From the clients' perspective, professional liability insurance provides the security of knowing that, in the event of an error, omission, or negligent act, they will be compensated. Without such assurance, clients may instead prefer to work with firms who are adequately covered.

Individual designers in a partnership or a limited company can be *personally* liable in claims initiated by clients and third parties. Should such claims be made, professional liability insurance will protect the designer's business or personal assets. The educated client will also know that a designer with insurance coverage will work harder for the economic advantage of the client than one who is operating without this security. Designers whose personal assets may be exposed to a claim may have a more conservative approach to design decisions; this may not necessarily be in the client's best interest.

All professional liability insurance is written on a claims-made basis; the insurance will only apply to claims actually made against the insured *during the policy period* and not to claims arising out of errors, omissions, or negligent acts committed after the term of the policy. The policy commonly requires either a written or verbal allegation of a breach in the rendering of service before a claim can be made. The mere reporting of a *potential* claim is insufficient to demand or expect coverage.

**Insurance on a
Claims-made
Basis**

To practice without professional liability insurance is to deny that there might ever be a claim, or that a client will ever be subject to loss due to an error, omission, or negligent act. The specter of the financial set-back of such a claim should convince designers of the good sense of such coverage.

Business runs on paper! The proper forms and the systems to use them allow designers to keep track of all functions; to keep finances in order; to record transactions; and to have on hand, at any time, a "snapshot" of the whole business.

**Keeping Track of
Business**

Business Papers Are an Extension of the Business and Should Be Designed, Too

Business forms should be developed in-house. The samples shown throughout this book should be used only as guides.

There are two types of forms: those which will be sent *out* of the office, to clients or contractors, for instance, and those for use *in* the office. The forms should be well-designed graphically as well as designed for the comfortable and efficient use of the persons involved. (If a computer will be used to record information, be cautious about letting a computer program define the design.)

The forms that go out of the office, including letterheads and envelopes, should be printed, and the firm's identifiable name and/or logo, address, and telephone number (and cable, fax, or toll-free 800 number) should be easy to locate and read. A type style that is readable, and one which respects the reader's eyesight by being larger than six-point, is desirable.

The forms for in-house use facilitate day-to-day information sharing and record-keeping.

Every form for business use must have a space for the date. It is best to avoid the strictly numerical style unless *day, month,* and *year* is printed on the form; 6/3 will invariably mean June 3 to one person and March 6 to another.

Fee Systems

3

Like other professionals, interior designers work for a fee–payment for particular expertise. The level of this fee relates to the designer's level of knowledge, experience, efficiency, and other factors.

In establishing the fee, creative staff salaries and the cost of doing business (*overhead*), plus a reasonable profit, must be taken into account.

Elements of the Fee

- office occupancy costs
- operating expenses
- business development costs
- professional costs
- miscellaneous costs

The Cost of Doing Business

Creative staff salaries are the basic wages paid to designers, draftsmen, project managers, and site supervisors. In addition, there are employee-related costs which include sick pay, vacation pay and holidays, unemployment insurance, payroll taxes, contributions for social security or government pension plans, and the cost of optional benefits such as private pension plan coverage, and medical, dental or other insurance. This "salary burden" may be 30 percent or more of the basic wage; thus, basic wages plus burden is the salary cost–or direct design personnel expense.

Office occupancy costs are the costs of maintaining an office, whether rented or owned. Included are rent, heat, light, air conditioning, maintenance, insurance, other applicable charges, and the cost of writing off or amortizing the capital expended in setting up the office, such as for furnishings and equipment.

Operating expenses include the salaries of support staff such as secretaries, typists, computer operators, receptionists; administrative and managerial staff; and resource librarians. These salaries, plus professional liability insurance, office and drafting supplies, printing, lawyers' and accountants' fees, interest, transportation, subscriptions, and losses due to bad debts all come under the heading of operating expenses.

Business development costs include promotion and advertising, and costs related to proposal submissions such as printing, meetings, consultations, and investigation. Satisfying long-time clients, whose requests must be met whether payment is forthcoming immediately or not, involves further costs. The rationale for this expense is simply to keep good clients happy when they expect short-term professional advice.

Professional costs are the costs of keeping up-to-date with the profession and might include such items as professional dues or sending people to committee and association meetings and continuing education conferences, which entail personnel costs as well as the expenses of travel and attendance. Productive time spent away from

design work is lost income and must be tallied in order to have an accurate idea of total professional costs.

"Miscellaneous" costs should not be a proportionately large figure in a budget, but firms must have sufficient reserves to cover occasional losses and unexpected expenses.

Overhead costs, added to designers' salaries, figure into fees charged. Depending on the size of the business, overhead can represent 130 percent of billable (productive) designers' salaries.

Calculating Profit

A design firm must make a reasonable profit, or there is no reason to stay in business and no opportunity to expand or grow. Therefore, bottom-line profit, figured as a percentage of total expected income, must be added to the overhead. What results is a multiplier of basic design wages, and this is usually around 2.5 or 3.0. Smaller firms have a lower multiplier (less overhead) while large firms may exceed a multiplier of 3.0.

The last thing to consider—and perhaps the most important—is that professional design service is a labor-intensive business; it is essential that the labor element (the design team's combined hourly wage multiplied by the time estimated for the project) be figured carefully. A few hours of unestimated overtime can wipe out all anticipated profit and even eat into overhead expenses. Detailed estimates and scrupulous recording of time is critical.

In an established firm, cost-accounting and estimating experts will be available to give accurate advice. A younger firm requires a good accounting system and accurate records to build a body of reference material for calculating fees.

Methods of Charging Design Fees

There are many ways to charge for design services. The fee may be stated in any one of the following ways or, occasionally, a combination of methods:
- hourly rate
- daily (or *per diem* rate)
- hourly or daily rate with fixed maximum
- fixed fee
- per-square-foot (or per-square-meter) fee
- percentage fee

Working on retainer, either short- or long-term, is another way of charging for services.

The designer and client agree to base compensation for the actual time expended by the designer/project staff, according to pre-determined **hourly rates**.

This method is particularly suited to a short-term agreement or when the nature of the work makes it difficult for the interior designer to calculate a final design fee. Charges vary for different members of staff; principals, senior designers, junior designers, and drafts-men are billed at different hourly rates. This method necessitates careful recording of time for accurate billing. Records should be available to the client for accounting purposes.

This system is workable for small projects–straight design consultation projects that could continue on a small scale over an indefinite period of time.

The hourly rate is determined by dividing the anticipated annual salary(ies) by the effective annual working hours, and then using the multipler. (Refer to box item.)

Establishing Hourly Rate

	Junior Designer	Senior Designer
Annual Hours	1410	1410
Annual Salary	$30,000.*	$60,000.*
Hourly Rate on Effective		
Annual Hours	$\frac{\$30,000.}{1410} = \$21.27$	$\frac{\$60,000.}{1410} = \$42.55$
Hourly Rate x Multiplier**	$21.27	$42.55
	x 2.5	x 2.5
	$53.18	$106.38
	$53./hour	$106./hour

* These are used as examples only; salaries vary considerably from region to region.
** Refer to page 40.

Evaluating Design Time

There are roughly 235 productive days in a year, after weekends, vacations, statutory holidays, and average days of sick leave are subtracted. In each day there are usually five to six productive hours–after deducting lunch hour, coffee breaks, non-productive phone calls–or approximately 1410 hours annually.

The charge for a senior designer's time will depend on several factors, such as experience, reputation, geographic location, and the economic status of the client. In a large firm, there must also be a charge for the principal of the firm, whether or not he or she is going to be directly involved in the design service. It is assumed and expected that this individual will be "on top of" the project, and that the expe-rience and reputation of the firm (embodied in the principal) will contribute to the success of the project. This is a legiti-mate assumption by clients, and remuneration for that person is therefore unquestioned. Charges for employees–junior designers, draftsmen, shoppers, project managers, and office support–will have to be calculated individually based on their annual salaries. These may be stated separately for each individual involved, or the various rates for the members of the design team may be added and averaged.

Before the hourly rate is fixed, the salary figures must be adjusted to include overhead and profit using the multi-plier method (refer to page 40). Established design firms generally use 3.0 as the multiplier. This factor for markup should not be applied without hard figures to back it up; first, because an essential part of business is knowing all overhead costs and, second, because clients deserve to clearly understand the markup.

On a project stretching over a considerable time period,

Establishing a Fixed Maximum Fee: An Example

Junior Designer
40 hours at $53 .... $2120.
Senior Designer
10 hours at $100. .... 1060.
$3180.
plus approximately 10%
for contingencies .... 320.
Maximum Fee $3500.

it is best to be clear at the outset about all charges. Direct personnel expenses should be stated, the overhead multiplier given, and a clause added to allow for adjustment of the personnel costs should salaries fluctuate or personnel change.

The daily (or per diem) rate is the rate for an effective six-hour workday based on the hourly rates as calculated above.

The hourly or daily rate with fixed maximum method requires the setting of a reasonable maximum fee, which should be the anticipated time required multiplied by the rate as established above, with a percentage added for contingencies. Accurate time records must be kept and the client must receive the benefit of any difference between actual time spent and the stated maximum.

Documentation

When using any of the above time-based fee systems, absolutely accurate records must be kept by all staff involved. Failure to record every minute of time–whether it is the designer's, the draftsman's, the shopper's, or others'–could result in loss for the firm. Padding time is an unethical practice. "Guesstimating" is unwise, not the practice of a professional firm. Appropriate time-recording forms are essential. (Refer to the time sheet, figure 1.)

The client is within his or her rights to ask for time-keeping documentation and may do so. The designer or firm must be in a position to provide scrupulously detailed records.

Generally, billings for service should be submitted throughout a job, although they may or may not be payable until the project is completed. This "progress billing" keeps the client up to date on the charges and diminishes the impact of the total cost.

The fixed fee method provides both the client and the designer with a definite billing figure at the beginning of the project. It is not recommended for use by inexperienced designers.

The fixed fee covers complete compensation for design services, exclusive of costs for specific expenses. It provides for all phases of design: concept, planning, detailing, and specifications of finishes and furnishings, but excludes shopping or purchasing on behalf of the client. It can be used only when the designer is able to determine the scope of the work, and can estimate time and effort with reasonable accuracy.

The fee is calculated based on the established hourly or daily rate and the time expected for completion. A percentage should also be added for contingencies.

This method may be used where the scope of the work is specific, where the amount of supervision is known, or where little or no supervision is required.

Although the fixed fee method appears simple, it has serious drawbacks as the designer is actually guessing the amount of time and work involved. Once committed to a fixed fee, the designer is bound by that figure. If the project entails more effort or time than anticipated, the designer will either lose money or will attempt to hurry the process, which may result in less-than-adequate work. This strategy may cost the designer in the long run; his or her reputation for good and thorough work may be adversely affected.

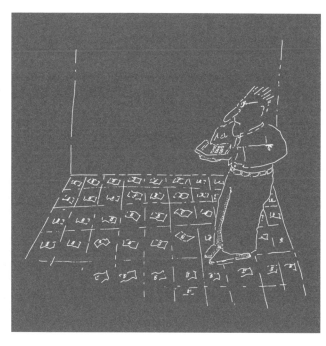

The per-square-foot (or per-square-meter) fee method divides a fixed fee (above) by the square footage (or square meters) of the area under design. It may be adaptable to specific services needed for large areas such as real estate promotion, stores and institutions, or to traffic-flow studies. Firms using this system must closely analyze prior jobs of a similar nature to arrive at an appropriate figure. This system is becoming increasingly common.

As a percentage of the total project cost, **the percentage fee** includes interior construction, finishing, installation, and furnishing costs. The percentage rate varies with the size of the project and must be based on a realistic budget. The fee is estimated after agreement between the client and interior designer as to how the project cost is to be established.

Determining Project Cost

The project cost is determined by one of the following methods:
- establishing a firm and reasonable cost at the outset
- establishing a project cost once all tenders have been received or orders placed
- totaling all actual invoices and other cost documents relating to the project

This system is used when purchasing budgets are comparatively large in relation to the time expended on professional services, including such projects as hospitals, hotels.

To define the cost of the work in a contract, refer to page 54, chapter 4.

As noted, fees for other consultants are excluded from the total on which the interior designer's fee is based.

The percentage fee also may be used for the client's costs for office improvements, or construction within a new building shell, for example, a percentage of total costs of partitions, lighting, electrical, and finishing materials.

Retainer

When a retainer is negotiated between a client and designer, the retainer payment is made to the interior designer prior to the commencement of work. The amount is kept outside the usual billings and is deducted from the final billing by the interior designer.

This system is used when a client wishes to engage the services of a designer as a consultant over a period of time, usually for one or more years, for example, for display homes or on-going maintenance work for corporations or institutions.

Long-Term Retainers

These are negotiated with the client for a predetermined period of time at fixed monthly payments. The interior designer renders services when and as required, with time expended in some relationship to the negotiated amount.

Vendor System

The fee systems previously described are based on professional fees for services rendered. Other systems involving purchase of goods, markup on manufacturer's costs, or on landed costs, describe the designer as *vendor*. Sometimes it is preferable to combine a professional fee system with a vendor system. Many jurisdictions require the establishment of a separate business for the vendor portion, including a business license and tax number.

This system, often used by interior designers working in the residential field, involves billing the client only for the retail price of furnishings and trade services. The difference between retail and wholesale prices to the trade becomes the design fee. This system is very popular with clients who feel that they are getting the design services *free*, and that their budget is being spent on tangible items such as flooring, wall finishes, and furnishings.

Choosing a Fee System

The methods of charging for professional design services have been developed over many decades. Each system can and does result in adequate payment. The designer's task is to figure out which system or combination is appropriate for each project. Clients are also part of the picture and their views may influence the decision.

Considerations When Quoting

The designer faced with quoting on a particular job must

▸ be familiar with the choice of fee systems available and how each works
▸ know the scope of the services required
▸ be aware of the client's budget
▸ have a thorough knowledge of the design firm's operations, design time available, overhead and income requirements, and the competition

Interior design is not a standardized professional service, nor is there a standard project. Different firms provide different services to different clients in different locales, so it is not surprising that fee schedules vary!

The scope of the work and the client's budget are the first factors to consider. Previous experience will help to determine what fee structure might be most suitable, particularly when a similar project has been completed satisfactorily and profitably.

When quoting, the availability of the designer to do the work is of course an important factor. If the designer is very much in demand, it may be possible to quote a higher-than-average hourly fee, whereas a designer who is looking for work might sell the services more reasonably. There is also the matter of competition. If several design firms are available, aggressive marketing and sharp pricing may secure the work. However, this situation should never result in "working for nothing."

- the credit rating of the client: will the client be able to pay for your services? will payment be delayed? (unknown client firms should provide credit information; otherwise, the designer should seek this information from appropriate agencies)
- the designated contact for the client: will one half of a couple make all the decisions or will the second person want equal time? will the designer be working with the company president, the office manager, or the board of directors?
- the availability of labor and materials: are they accessible or must they be transported to the site? are finishes and furnishings locally available?
- distance: is travel time between the job and the designer's office a factor for the design team?

Contracts

4

In general terms, a contract is a binding agreement between two or more parties. In business terms, it usually involves the provision of some type of service for a set period of time for a fee. All parties to a contract have rights and responsibilities.

A contract to provide design services may be fairly simple or very complicated. The extent of complexity depends on the scope of the work to be done. Writing the contract therefore involves detailed preparation. Many items must be considered (see the following page).

Any contract signed by the parties involved is legally binding. Less formal agreements backed up by letters or notes of conversations are also binding but are fraught with problems in interpretation–any disputes will invariably involve legal wrangling and therefore time and money.

Written Contracts Make Good Business Sense

Good business practice dictates that a written contract that outlines the terms of agreement between the designer (or design firm) and the client is advised. Each party to the agreement should retain a copy of the contract–dated, signed, and witnessed. It is also essential that any such contract be clear and unambiguous. Lengthy, detailed contracts eliminate ambiguity, however, they need not be full of legal jargon; plain English is always preferred.

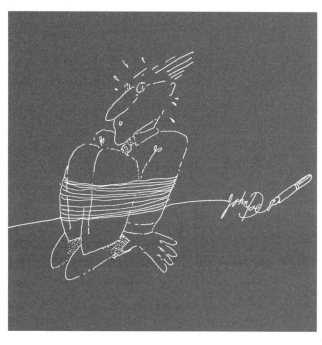

The finished contract should be reviewed by the designer's lawyer and project insurer prior to signing. If one of the standard forms of contracts (see Appendix) is adapted with even minimal changes, check it with legal counsel to assure that clauses specifying both the client's and the designer's responsibilities apply in the geographical location of practice. Remember that clients will also be checking with lawyers.

It is also worth noting that one party's ignorance of contracts will be apparent to another who understands them. The "smart party" may or may not be sympathetic with the other's lack of knowledge, and may even be tempted to use such ignorance to take unfair advantage.

One final point: the contract should be initiated by the designer, not the client.

First Steps

Assume discussions have taken place between the designer and the proposed client, and both are ready to undertake the project.

Before entering into a contract make sure to review the following:
- the scope of the work
- the client's background and reputation
- the interior design firm's capabilities

Some pertinent questions to answer before writing the contract fall under the heading of "exactly what services are to be performed?" To establish these, consider the following:

The Scope of the Work

▸ If the building (or space) is new, is it finished and, if so, what is included in the finishing?

▸ If the building is existing, are the plans available or does the space require on-site measuring?

▸ Is special detailing in millwork and cabinet work required?

▸ Will construction work be tendered by the design firm?

▸ What furniture is to be reused and what new furnishings are required?

▸ Is some furniture to be custom-designed?

▸ Will fully detailed furniture specifications be required?

▸ Are any other consultants involved? What are their responsibilities?

▸ When does the project need to be completed? Is the completion date realistic? Will the project require overtime in order to meet the deadline?

▸ How much supervision and installation time will be involved?

▸ Will the designer be responsible for checking invoices for payment?

▸ What services are *not* required? If some services are explicitly exempted, are these exclusions outlined in the contract?

The Client Profile

It is important to know exactly who the client is, who the contact will be, and whether that person (or those persons) will also be responsible for payment for the design services. To clarify these points:

▸ Establish the client's background insofar as financial capability, reputation in the business world (if applicable), and credit standing are concerned.

▸ Establish whether the client is a single owner, a partnership, or a business entity such as a corporation. If the client is a company, there must be an authorized contact with whom to deal, and the funding for the project must be assured by the principals of the firm.

▸ Assess whether the client will usually accept the design concepts or whether there is a likelihood of changes in mid-project.

▸ Establish whether the project is to be completed as a whole, or is to be divided into stages.

The Design Firm's Capabilities

It is not an absolute given that every project opportunity should be undertaken. Before participating, several points must be considered:

▸ Do the necessary skills exist in-house or will outside consultants have to be retained?

▸ Is there time to do the work within regular working hours, or will the project require overtime?

▸ Does the project fit the firm's business plan or is it being considered simply to keep staff busy?

▸ Is it convenient to work on the project? If, for example, the firm's business consists mainly of urban stores and offices, an elaborate summer-home project forty miles away may be appealing, but the impact the travel time necessitated will have on other work must be considered.

Oral agreements have elements of risk and should usually be avoided. If an oral agreement must be considered, it should only apply to a very limited job, such as a small residential assignment. At the very least, confirm the understanding of the scope of services, the schedule, and the fee in an informal letter to the client. Confirm any subsequent quotations or orders in writing and keep accurate time records. If a client finds something not to his or her liking in such a letter of understanding, the designer will certainly be notified! Lack of response *may* be taken as consent, but the client may later claim not having received the letter or not having understood it. Prior correspondence will certainly help in any dispute, but an oral agreement is not considered a binding and legal contract, and it will be the designer's responsibility to prove that an understanding with the client exists.

Contractual Concerns

Oral Agreements

Becoming familiar with legal documents and their formats is time well spent. Read leases, service contracts for the car, insurance policies, banking papers, and product guarantees–studying them for their content and major points.

Notice how words are used to ensure fairness to both parties and protection for the party issuing the document. When a contract's purpose is understood, the format and mechanics make basic good sense.

Letters of Agreement

If, with the above-mentioned letter, an extra copy is enclosed and the client's signature is requested on both copies (initials on each page), with the return of one copy to the designer, then a letter of agreement has been created. While this form of contract may be brief and ambiguous, it *is* legally recognized. Protection may be further assured by excerpting pertinent clauses from a standard contract and inserting them into the letter of agreement.

Contracts

A proper contract is good business. Whether you are dealing with business firms or with residential clients, a businesslike approach is usually valued. Sign the contract before any design work starts, or soon thereafter, depending on the scale of the project.

All decisions regarding the project will flow from the contract: the work, the schedule, the financial issues, and means of arbitration. A well-written contract covers all the bases.

Although "disputes" and "conflicts" have been mentioned many times, it is not the intent of this book to instill an adversarial tone to this phase of business. The designer and the client intend to accomplish something together, and this goal should be uppermost as the contract is prepared. All the facets of the work, as understood and discussed between the designer and the client, are written down as succinctly as possible. The contract is a record for both parties and, more often than not, becomes the agreed-upon base for the buying/selling of professional expertise.

The Form of the Contract

All contracts follow a certain set form. All have *first matter, the body of the contract, other matter,* and *signatories.*

The First Matter
- indicates the number of copies
- notes the date and the location of the contract writing
- identifies the parties
- states the subject of the agreement

The Body of the Contract
- states the location and physical parameters of the work
- has details of the professional design services to be rendered including purchasing arrangements, supervisory responsibilities, and exclusions to the work
- states the fee arrangement and schedule of payments
- includes the time-frame of the project
- clarifies issuance of change orders

Other Matter
- describes compensation for out-of-pocket expenses
- defines third-party services
- includes disclaimers
- defines rights
- defines arbitration of disputes
- describes assignments

Signatories

The contract ends with witnessed signatures, the signing date, and the company seals (if applicable). Each page of the contract as well as any insertions, deletions, and/or corrections must be initialed by all parties to the contract.

The signed original should be kept in a safe place, preferably with the design firm's lawyer. For working purposes, photocopies may be made, with every page clearly marked as a copy.

First Matter

Contracts are most often drawn up in duplicate, unless there are more than two responsible parties to the contract. There must be a signed, legally acceptable copy for each party.

The date shown in the first matter is the date on which the contract was drawn up. The location indicates the legal jurisdiction of the agreement. Unless stated otherwise, the contract will be interpreted by the law of that location.

The parties to the contract are the designer and the client. They should be clearly identified by name and address, and after each a phrase such as "hereinafter referred to as the Owner [or Tenant, or Company, or...]." The designer may be a sole proprietor, or a representative of any one of the other types of practice discussed. The business arrangement dictates in whose name the contract is written and who is to sign. The client's identity must be described. The least complicated client for contract purposes is an individual who owns and occupies the property where the design service is to be rendered.

If residential work is being undertaken for a married couple or any number of individuals cohabiting a space, it is advisable to write the contract in all of their names. This is protection for the designer in case of separation of the client parties. Each signature implies responsibility for the fee.

If commercial work is being undertaken, the client may act on his or her own behalf, or contracts may be signed by a person or persons unknown. (Government contracts in Canada are drawn up with "Her Majesty the Queen[!]…is in right of" the particular government department and location involved.) If a local signing authority is needed, this should be stipulated in the *other matter* along with an outline of limitations on their spending and authority.

The Subject of the Agreement

The *subject of the agreement* in the first matter is a very brief statement, such as "to render professional interior design services as hereinafter described." Or it may go into further general detail, such as:

"The interior designer shall perform the following services: programming; design concept; design development; contract documentation; contract administration. Upon the request of the client, the designer will furnish in writing preliminary estimates of the cost of materials, articles or work hereunder, but the designer does not guarantee the accuracy of such estimates."

The wording in this section of the contract is not intended as a comprehensive statement; it merely indicates the broad content that follows.

The Body of the Contract
Site Location

Indicate clearly the premises involved. Locate using address, square footage, and the borders of the space. Be specific!

Details of the Design Service

The nature and scope of interior design services vary extensively; they should be carefully detailed during preliminary discussions, particularly with clients who have not previously worked with designers. Incorporate all planned activity into the contract, documenting specific obligations. This clarifies the services that will be rendered by the designer, as opposed to those services that might be required from third parties in the completion of the overall project.

The following checklist should be used to flag those items that the contract will specify in detail regarding the tasks and the subject areas involved.

Programming

- Identify and analyze client's and users' needs and goals.
- Evaluate the existing documentation and the condition of the premises, including furnishings and equipment, space allocation, and other attributes of the existing environment.
- Assess the project's resources and limitations, both physical and financial.
- Identify life, safety, and code requirements.

▶ Consider site issues, such as location and access.
▶ Prepare project schedule and work plan.
▶ Develop budgets for the interior construction and furnishings.
▶ Analyze the design objectives and spatial requirements.
▶ Develop preliminary space planning and furniture layouts.
▶ Determine the need for consultants and other specialists if required by professional practice or for regulatory approval; make recommendations to the client and act as coordinator.
▶ Investigate requirements for regulatory approval.
▶ Organize information for client discussion and approval.

Design Concept

▶ Formulate the preliminary plans and three-dimensional design concepts that are appropriate to the program's budget and that describe the character, function, and aesthetic of the project.
▶ Prepare image boards.
▶ Present the conceptual design and preliminary cost estimates to the client for discussion and approval.

Design Development

▶ Develop and refine the approved conceptual design.
▶ Research and consult with jurisdictional authorities regarding building and life-safety codes, applicable health and liquor regulations, and so on.
▶ Communicate with necessary specialists/consultants.
▶ Develop the art, accessories, and graphic/signage program.
▶ Develop and present for client review and approval the final design recommendations for space planning, furnishings, fixtures, millwork, and all interior surfaces, including lighting, electrical, and communication requirements.
▶ Refine budget estimate.
▶ Prepare a presentation to the client for discussion and approval, using a variety of media such as plans, perspectives, renderings, color and material boards, photographs, and models.

Contract Documentation

▶ Prepare the working drawings and related schedules for interior construction, materials, finishes, furnishings, fixtures, and equipment for client approval.
▶ Coordinate the professional services of specialty consultants and licensed practitioners in the technical areas of mechanical, electrical, and load-bearing design and construction, as required for regulatory approvals.
▶ Identify qualified builders.
▶ Prepare the bid documents, construction specifications, and furnishing specifications.
▶ Issue addenda as necessary.
▶ Collect and review the bids.
▶ Assist the client in awarding contracts.

Contract Administration

▶ Administer contract documents as the client's agent.
▶ Confirm that the required permits are obtained.
▶ Monitor the contractors'/suppliers' progress.
▶ As necessary, issue proposed change notices, change orders.
▶ Conduct periodic site visits and inspections.
▶ Review and approve shop drawings and samples.
▶ Oversee the installation of furnishings, fixtures, and equipment.
▶ Review the invoices and issue certificates of payment.
▶ Prepare a list of deficiencies.

- Make final inspection.
- Prepare the equipment and maintenance manual.
- Monitor the project through the guarantee period.
- Terminate the contracts.

- Review and evaluate the design solution after project completion.
- If required by client, conduct a post-occupancy evaluation survey.

Evaluation

Before the contract is written, some of the above points can be clarified by the addition of detail. For instance, the development of the design concept may be described as an *exploratory phase*. This term reassures clients that their ideas will be considered–that flexibility is part of the design process.

If areas need attention, but have not been discussed or requirements specified, the designer may describe services that others could provide, or additional helpful services the designer could provide at extra cost.

It is best to elaborate on the designer's supervisory services; without a description, clients may expect overall day-to-day supervision. The contract should state what phases of the work will be personally supervised by the designer, thus avoiding the client's expectancy of exclusive attention to this one project.

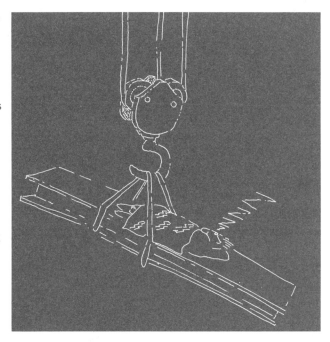

Based on the discussion of fee systems in chapter 3, the fee is written into the contract. Through discussion and assessment of the scope of work with the client, a fee system and figures will have been agreed upon. The total fee should be estimated by using a fee estimation worksheet.

The Fee

An example of wording for an hourly-rate fee follows. (Wording for a daily-rate based fee would be similar, except the *per hour* changes to *per day*.)

Time-Based Fees

"The Client shall pay to the Designers, for services rendered, a fee based upon a time rate, as hereinafter defined:
Principals–$/per hour (day)
Senior Designers–$/per hour (day)
Junior Designers–$/per hour (day)
Billable Support Staff–$/per hour (day)
Draftsmen–$/per hour (day)"

Wording for an hourly-rate fee with a maximum total would simply have a phrase added, such as: "...not to exceed a maximum total fee of $15,000."

A further statement clarifies the terms of payment and the obligation to carefully record time spent on the project:

"The Designers' fees as outlined above shall be payable monthly, on receipt of itemized monthly statements. The

Designers shall keep weekly time-analysis records and submit same to Client with the statements."

Percentage-Based Fees

Example of wording for a percentage fee arrangement:

"The Client shall pay to the Designer for services rendered a fee of _____ percent of the cost of the work as hereinafter defined, the cost of which is estimated at $_____.

a) thirty percent (30%) thereof, based on the estimated figure, upon acceptance of this contract;

b) forty percent (40%) thereof, based upon the estimated figure, upon the completion of working drawings, specifications, and color schemes;

c) the balance thereof from time to time thereafter, in proportion to the services rendered by the Designer, by additional payments to the Designer on his [or her] requisition, until the total amount of all the payments under this clause shall equal the said fee based upon the cost of the work."

An example of breakdown of fees calculated on the percentage basis, using 10 percent for the first $100,000. and 5 percent for the cost over $100,000. might be as follows:

Stage of Services	Percentage Fee on first $100,000.	Percentage Fee on portion over $100,000.
Programming	1.5	.75
Design Concept	2.0	1.00
Design Development	2.5	1.25
Contract Documentation	2.5	1.25
Contract Administration	1.5	.75
	10.0	5.00

Alternate wording for a percentage fee arrangement might be:

"...a fee based upon a percentage of the cost of the work, as hereinafter defined:

The fee shall be _____ percent (_____%) based on the first $_____ of the cost of work and _____ percent (_____ %) based on the cost of work over and above $_____."

Suggested wording following one of the above choices:

"Eighty-five percent (85%) of the fees shall be paid periodically as the Designer's services are performed. Fifteen percent (15%) of the fees shall be paid upon completion of this contract. These percentages may differ according to the local custom of various jurisdictions.

It is further understood that the provision for payment of the fees in installments is solely for convenience and does not measure and is not intended to measure the value of the Designer's service up to the time that payments are provided for."

Defining the Cost of the Work

The cost of the work must be carefully defined. An example of wording is:

"The cost of the work shall be the actual cost to the Client of the work and of all additions or alterations thereto, and shall include suppliers' profits and expenses, shipping charges, installation charges, insurance premiums, and taxes other than income taxes, but shall not include fees or other payments to the Designer or to any architect, engineer, or other professional consultant or the cost of continuous on-site inspection of the work. Should labor, materials, or furnishings be supplied by the Client below their market cost or should old materials be reused, cost is to be interpreted as the cost of all labor, materials, or furnishings necessary to complete the work as such cost would have been if all materials had been new and if all labor had been paid for at market prices current when the work was ordered."

A fee may also be based on the square footage involved and contract wording could be similar to the example above, substituting "a fee of _____ per square foot based on the total of _____ square feet."

Per-Square-Foot (or Per-Square-Meter) Fees

If any other fee system (or combination of systems) has been discussed and agreed upon, this should be written clearly and concisely into the contract.

Other Fee-Related Issues

Whatever fee system is used, the contract must state how the billings will be rendered and how payments should be made. Some invoices state that payment is to be made on demand, "when rendered," others ask for quick payment in, for example, seven days. While this is appropriate for residential work, it is unrealistic for commercial clients who pay monthly. It is reasonable and usual to expect payment thirty days after billing; if a late payment charge or monthly interest fee is charged, this should be stated in the contract. Also, if billing over an extended period of two or more years, an inflation factor may be built in.

A definite indication of the time frame discussed and agreed upon by the designer and client should be written into the contract. Bear in mind that this is a legally binding document; do not promise more than can be delivered. However, a clause that absolves the designer from responsibility for unforeseen scheduling problems should be added for protection.

Time Frame

All too often designers fail to indicate when and how a contract is to end; this should be stated in specific terms.

It is important to outline the designer's position on changes, additional work not included in the contract, or payment requirements in the event of abandonment of the project. Possible wording might be:

Changes

"If, after a definite scheme has been approved, the Client requires additions or alterations thereto or services additional to those required hereunder, the Client will pay the Designer a reasonable additional fee. If any work undertaken by the Designer pursuant to this contract is abandoned in whole or in part by the Client, or by the Designer, the Client will pay the designer a reasonable fee for his [or her] services in connection with such work."

The stage-of-services breakdown, listed under *Percentage-Based Fees* (page 54) may be used as a guide in calculating such a fee.

The contract should include the designer's position on various ancillary matters. These are as important to the contract as the matters of work and fee; they cover areas where disputes are liable to arise if details are not clearly outlined before the work has progressed.

Other Matter

Preliminary analysis of the scope of work will indicate whether–and what kind of–other expenses are likely to be incurred.

Compensation for Out-of-Pocket Expenses

acts

This clause may be worded as follows, adding other specific items as applicable:

"The Client shall also pay or reimburse or indemnify the Designer upon his [or her] written requisition for all expenses or liability necessarily and reasonably incurred in connection with the work with respect to the following items:

a) when authorized hereunder, the purchasing of materials and articles and the letting of contracts for work and services

b) the cost of transportation and living expenses incurred by the Designer or employees while traveling in discharge of duties connected with the work if it is outside of the city

c) provision of continuous on-site inspection of the work if the same is requested in writing by the Client

d) telephone and other communication charges made in the interests of the Client

e) cost of prints, photography, renderings, models, mock-ups, and other reproductions and perspectives"

Third-Party Services

When the project requires the services of consultants or other third parties (such as architects; engineers; landscape architects; heating, plumbing, electrical, air-conditioning, or other mechanical contractors) the method whereby these services are to be obtained and reimbursed should be spelled out. This may be worded, with specific references to third parties if known, as follows:

"If the Client should desire to bring in consultants on the work or any part of it, they must be approved by the Interior Designer. The Designer will then collaborate with the consultants and the fees and expenses of such consultants will be paid by the Client."

Disclaimers

The designer must never assume responsibility for the work of others (third parties) or for the quality of materials or articles purchased.

Wording to this effect should be added to the contract:

"The Designer shall not warrant or be responsible for the quality of materials or articles purchased or installed in the Client's premises or for the structural condition of said premises or for the acts, work, or services of any employee or contractor of the Client. The Designer shall keep records and render a full and complete accounting as to all materials and articles purchased or work or services contracted by him [or her] together with any and all sums received or paid by him [or her] pursuant hereto."

In addition to the above, a clause may be added indicating the client's responsibility in this area, such as:

"The Client shall deliver to the Designer as received all bills, estimates, invoices, orders, and other documents relating to the work or the cost thereof and give the Designer such further information as he [or she] may require in that regard. The Client shall not deduct from any payments due to the Designer under this agreement any amounts which he [or she] may be entitled to charge or claim against any employee or contractor of the Client."

Rights

Ownership of the design and related documents should be established. The design belongs to the designer, and ownership can be stipulated as follows:

"All designs, samples, drawings, specifications, and other documents shall be the property of the Designer whether the work for which they are made is executed or not, and shall not be used, executed, reproduced, or copied, except in relation to the contemplated work, without the written consent of the Designer."

The designer may also wish to clarify the right to photograph and publish the design and the finished work for promotional purposes. An acknowledgment of the client's right to privacy should be added in this case, stating that the client's name and location of the work will not be revealed without written permission.

Arbitration of Disputes

The designer must be aware of the availability of dispute-settling methods in the locale of practice. Throughout the United States, the designer may wish to rely on the *Rules of the American Arbitration Association*. In other areas, check with legal counsel regarding accepted methods of dispute settlement.

A general statement may be written into the contract as follows, with particulars inserted:

"All matters in dispute under this agreement shall be submitted to arbitration at the request of either party.

No one shall be nominated or act as arbitrator who is in any way financially interested in the conduct of the work or in the business affairs of either party.

The laws of _____ shall govern the arbitration.

The decision of the arbitrator or arbitrators shall be final and binding upon the parties and this covenant to submit to arbitration is to be construed as an integral part of this agreement between the parties."

Assignment

To cover the possibility of either party being unable to fulfill the terms of the contract (for example, sale of a business, designer's overload, ill health) a simple sentence of assignment should be added. Suggested wording is:

"Neither party hereto shall assign his [or her] interest in and to this agreement without the written consent of the other."

In closing, unless there are clauses to be added that are specific to the project, the contract should provide spaces for signatures, a witness for each party, and a date line.

Guarantee of Fee

In some cases, the designer may have reason to ask for a guarantor of the fee. For instance, this may occur in the case of a fledgling company having their first offices designed. The company itself may be too new to have a track record for credit purposes, and it is not unusual for the principal or principals of the client firm, or a third party, to give a personal guarantee of payment.

Such a clause follows the signatures and may state:

"In consideration of the Designer entering into the above contract, I hereby guarantee payment by the Client of any and all sums falling due thereunder."

This guarantee is then signed, witnessed, and dated.

Standard Contract Forms

Designers are aware of the availability of many standard contract forms. Sources for examples of standard contracts may be found in the bibliography of this book. If these forms accurately reflect the types of work undertaken, they may be easy to use and are worth investigating and adapting.

Occasionally, a client will offer to write the contract. This may be attractive to the designer but such a contract must be read very carefully to ascertain that the designer's rights are safeguarded.

Review

The final step in any contract negotiation is to have legal counsel read and approve of the contract. Particularly with first ventures in professional practice, it is infinitely "better to be safe than sorry."

Marketing Design Services

Marketing

Marketing is a generic, all-inclusive term for the movement of goods and services from producers to consumers. Producers (in this case, interior designers) have to know the market in order to sell their commodity (interior design service) to consumers (clients). This involves an understanding of the clients'/users' desires, attitudes, and circumstances in order to determine which design services are saleable and the character of the marketing required.

Potential clients must be aware of the "commodity" available before they can be motivated to buy. Because of this, the task of professional interior designers is to promote the benefits of their services, both general and specific, to particular consumers, and to encourage their use.

Designers must realize the importance of this business aspect of their profession. They have to "get their foot in the door" to convince prospective clients that the services they are selling are worthwhile and that their particular service is the best value for the money.

The Fundamentals of Marketing

The question of *how* to market anything has been answered over time, and a body of marketing fundamentals, or basic principles, has been developed. These common-sense guides may be applied to the selling of design services, just as they are used to market other goods and services.

The fundamentals of marketing are concerned with
- identifying the opportunity
- identifying the service to be marketed
- identifying the decision-makers
- identifying the influences
- determining the motivators
- admitting constraints and providing solutions
- developing the marketing tools
- developing public relations, promotions, and personal contacts
- implementing the plan of action

The opportunity to apply the fundamentals of marketing exists when
- the designer is looking for a position
- the design firm is looking for a project
- the designer has a solution that fits a specific market

Each step of a marketing program requires careful planning. The effectiveness of basic market research is in proportion to the time and effort put into it.

It is possible to contract out all or part of this work. If the expense can be afforded, study several marketing firms

Planning a Marketing Program

Marketing professionals have developed some rules-of-thumb that are helpful in planning the marketing program:

- Out of every ten contacts, one solid prospect should result.
- For every five presentations to prospects, one job may be expected.
- The budget for promotion should be 3 to 5 percent of gross income; some consultants suggest 5 to 10 percent. New businesses probably need to spend 10 percent; the predetermined amount should be included in annual budgets.
- Business development time is about the same as that required for human reproduction—nine months is an average lead time. Allow at least that much time before expecting concrete results from a sales effort.

before signing a contract. Discover the type of research that they do, ask for number of employees, fees, and references.

Identifying the Opportunity

Designers and design firms must become adept at identifying where there are needs for interior designers.

Some opportunities may be found by responding to
- ads in the career sections of newspapers
- job listings in trade magazines
- announcements for zoning variations
- financial developments in a previously quiet sector
- the needs of a specific client

Identifying the Service

The design firm must know its own capabilities in order to clarify *what* to promote. In the following checklist, marketable services fall under several broad headings:

Professional Knowledge and Skills

- fundamentals of design: analysis, space planning and programming, design of interior spaces, and an understanding of other and related disciplines of environmental design
- technical knowledge of structure (with emphasis on interior construction), building systems, equipment, components, and products
- communication skills: translation of ideas into drawings and specifications
- awareness and analytical skills: understanding the "people needs" that can be met by sensitive design
- design sensitivity: creative and conceptual abilities combined with technical proficiency

Personal Representation of the Profession

- ability to articulate design information using listening skills, interview techniques, oral and written communication
- knowledge of business methods and ethical conduct
- knowledge of the profession
- interest in other occupations
- development of a positive personal image

Knowledge Gained Through Experience

- in internship
- in interior design
- in related job experiences
- in day-to-day living

Specialization

- areas of particular interest and specialization

In order to target the marketing activity, the designer must identify decision-makers. They may be either persons who recognize a need for professional services, or persons who need help but don't recognize it. In either case, they may be
- one or more individuals
- a committee
- middle-management personnel
- senior executives within a corporation

Identifying the Decision-Makers

The successful design firm is aware of the economic factors of the times. Consider
- the population and economic status of an area
- the projected growth and development of the area
- the reasons for growth

Identifying the Market Influences

Select appropriate companies–ones that appear to need design services. Question what would motivate these companies to use interior design services or, in particular, to hire your firm.

Determining the Motivators

Analysis may be based on the following:
- the company's needs fall within your area of specialization
- the company would save money, space, time, and so on, if design services were applied
- the company would gain from better employee relationships through staff satisfaction with their surroundings, and would also find improved efficiency within the working environment
- whether the potential client can easily pay for the services, or needs to be convinced that it is economically feasible to hire the services
- the life-safety factors involved that are of prime importance to the consumer/client/users
- considerations for the aged and/or the handicapped

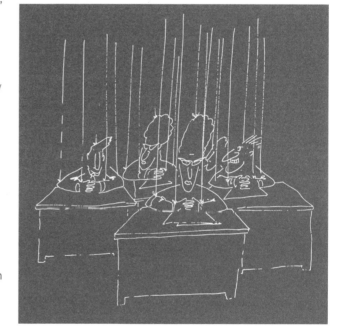

Analysis should conclude with the questions: Is the prospect interested in the services? If there is no immediate interest, how is the prospect to be motivated into realizing that the services are needed?

In the process of assessing the design "product" to be sold, it is necessary to admit constraints, that is, to be realistic about the scope of services to be offered. The capabilities/limitations of the individual or design firm must be well known in order to determine the employment possibilities.

Admitting Constraints

This will involve
- the present and potential capabilities and specialties
- any weaknesses and/or limitations
- the general practice mix–and what is missing from it
- the principals, professionals, technicians, and support staff

Knowledge of the Design Firm

Scope of Services

- the predetermined range of services required for a prospective project
- allowance or preparation for modification to this range of services
- realistic goals based on the ability to handle the scale of a particular project
- a desirable geographic coverage area
- knowledge of the competition, both present and anticipated

Developing the Tools

The Name, Logo, Business Card, and Brochures

The basic image-making tools for any firm are the *name* (possibly incorporating the designers' own names) and the *logo*. The graphic interpretation of these two identifiers is then used on business cards, brochures, letterheads, and so on.

The *business card* is the briefest statement of the designers' availability to work. While designers may feel competent in devising their own cards, it is prudent to take all information and ideas to a graphic designer who will add professional expertise in the selection of type style and paper stock.

To be effective, a *brochure* should be professionally designed. A good graphic designer will be able to specify the most economic size, shape, and method of printing, and will probably save money in the long run. A brochure contains the company's name, address, telephone and fax numbers, and information about the particular skills and expertise being offered. It may also contain photographs of the designers' drawings. (See *Elements of a Good Brochure* on page 65.) Consider using a professional writer whose skills will guarantee a well-prepared text.

All related business forms should be part of the design package. Black ink on white paper can be reproduced inexpensively, but any one color may be used effectively and at little upcharge. Consider screens and other devices the graphic designer may suggest to make the forms more functional and more interesting.

Proposal Guidelines

When developing a proposal document, consider the following components:

- introduction (a brief letter to the prospective client, referring to the specifics that motivated this particular presentation, directed to the right person, correctly addressed, and fully referenced)
- profile of the design firm
- terms of reference and scope of services
- critical path
- proposed agreement
- associations, joint ventures, subcontracts
- staff experience
- visual aids (charts, graphs, past projects)
- compensation/fee schedule

Visuals, Drawings, Letters

Promotional tools can expand to fit almost any budget. Some to consider are *visuals*, such as a slide presentation or video featuring completed projects, programming methodology, and forms (assure *quality* of visuals and prepare for handling, transporting, and using equipment); using an excellent set of completed *working drawings*; and *letters*, which include a general introduction of the design firm and the promotional package, an indication of interest in the client's project, and references from previous clients that document their satisfaction.

In all letters, be sure that names, titles, and addresses are correct. Use wide margins, be brief (80 to 120 words is suggested), and be sure the signature is noticeable and memorable.

These are summary sheets for quick reference that include basic project data such as

▶ client, building, location
▶ size: square feet/meters, number of floors
▶ costs: total, per square foot/meter, relation to budget (client's permission is usually required to quote prices)
▶ unique elements, such as a new partition-system design
▶ time frame: length of time of project; was project on schedule?
▶ personnel involved: firm staff, outside consultants, contractors
▶ client contact: include telephone and fax numbers, correct address, alternative phone number
▶ other consultants: listing of professional consultants–where, when, and how they would be used in association with the client's project

Proposals

Proposals are developed by a design firm to set forth the unique capabilities of the firm and the services being offered for a specific project. The proposal outlines how the design firm would proceed on the client's specific project. (See *Proposal Guidelines,* page 64.)

A first-class proposal is a major investment of business development funds. Preparation should be undertaken selectively and with a commitment to compile and produce a truly professional, responsive document.

Some basic questions to consider before going ahead with a proposal include:

▶ Does the prospective client have the necessary funds to pay for the required services?
▶ Does the prospective client really need this particular firm? How many competitors (and of what quality) will the design firm face?
▶ Does this design office have the expertise to successfully compete against the probable competition?
▶ Is the geographical area of the proposed project of real interest to the firm?
▶ Does this design firm have the required staff available and the financial capability to handle the job?

Elements of a Good Brochure
In the development of a brochure for an interior design firm, consider the following:

Marketing Purpose
▶ to sell interior design services in a professional manner

Content
▶ a short profile of the company and its history
▶ an outline of the services available
▶ information on design and support personnel
▶ a list of completed projects/satisfied clients

Good Design
▶ imaginative use of paper, type style, color, and so on
▶ contemporary design techniques

Comprehensive Graphics
▶ titles and headings for impact and easy reference
▶ legible graphics
▶ fidelity to the company image being established

Comprehensive Text
▶ clear
▶ brief
▶ contemporary tone
▶ correct spelling, punctuation, and grammar
▶ good use of headings and subheadings to highlight main points

Cover
▶ meaningful, provocative

Photographs and Artwork
▶ photos, illustrations of completed projects
▶ relaxed photographs of staff and associates at work (black and white photos are as effective as color and less expensive)

Public Relations, Promotion, and Personal Contact

6

Marketing design services is a three-pronged activity consisting of
▶ public relations–becoming known as a reputable interior design professional or firm
▶ promotion–advertising interior design service to a broad target audience
▶ personal contact–selling specific design services to selected prospective clients through proposals and presentations

All three activities must be undertaken simultaneously and must be ongoing. Ideally, personal contact builds on promotion that has been based on good public relations. It is easier, though not essential, if all three aspects of marketing are working continually.

Public Relations

The aim of public relations activity is to shape public opinion in favor of the designer. In order to enjoy the beneficial effects of good PR, the designer/firm must be seen in a positive light. This requires *indirect self-promotion*, that is, the acquisition of a good reputation through means other than direct promotion–influencing people's opinions without attempting to sell them design services. For instance, the principal of a firm who serves on the board of a cultural organization presumably is known as a concerned citizen who is willing to donate time and effort to bettering the community. (How these commitments are fulfilled dictates the actual opinion formed of the individual.)

> The firm must become known to its
> ▶ professional peers
> ▶ resources: suppliers and tradespeople
> ▶ potential clients

Depending on the business the designer most wants to attract, the *positive light* may be friendly and approachable, innovative and creative, businesslike and competent, dramatic, or simply efficient, or any chosen combination of attributes. It is important to have in mind exactly what you want people to think and feel before embarking on public relations activity.

The designer should meet and get to know fellow interior design professionals, architects, landscape architects, industrial designers, educators in the field, local media personalities, and all pertinent suppliers, manufacturers, and sales representatives, civic employees who deal with the building trades, local elected officials or bureaucrats who have authority in the designer's areas of work, contractors, and workshop personnel. Establish a good file with names, addresses, and phone numbers, and record comments or notes. The focus should be on knowing these people for ease of communication and also to *become* known. The designer's friendliness, interest in others, and respect for their work will be remembered.

Public relations planning falls into two categories: first, planning specific targeted activity, and second, planning how to take advantage of opportunities as they arise. Both need careful forethought.

A good public relations campaign
▸ identifies the result–or positive image–desired
▸ identifies the audience(s)
▸ makes plans and seeks out appropriate opportunities or occasions for the PR activity
▸ carries out the plan

Identifying the Desired Image

If the designer has a chosen specialty, a particular reputation is not difficult to imagine. Basically, it requires brainstorming activity–putting yourself in a client's shoes–to come up with the particular attributes most likely to be attractive to the client.

Identifying the Audience

Based on the designer's type of work and the image to be shaped, the next planning exercise is to pinpoint the potential client audience for public relations activity. Usually PR is aimed at specific audiences–health-care professionals, decision-makers within the hotel industry, homeowners–sometimes the same PR will reach several audiences, or there may be a cumulative effect.

One specific activity is involvement in professional associations, which are perceived as having good ethics. This reputation may then be ascribed to the designer and/or firm through association. The broadest impact can be made if the designer is active and visible and uses the association's initials wherever possible. Membership also offers the opportunity to be involved in community service and to be on referral lists for projects.

The designer should also research and assess various organizations. Involvement in high-profile public service such as the arts, historic preservation, social service, or environmental concerns will be of potential value. Both special-interest groups and large organizations should be assessed for their eventual business potential.

Assessing Involvement in Community Organizations

Points to consider are:
▸ their membership: are the existing members (or members of their boards of directors) possible clients?
▸ the reputation of the organization: is it well regarded in the community? does it have a good PR program of its own? does it publish a newsletter or sponsor public lectures?

- the compatibility level: do the interests and activities of the organization fit the designer's interests?
- the involvement level expected: will being a member of the organization or its board provide sufficient contact with the target audience or will it be necessary to become more involved? (the designer must be cautious of over-commitment)

Becoming involved with a volunteer organization is usually not difficult, but it does require genuine interest and, most important, time and the ability to make a commitment. Becoming a member of cultural or recreational organizations requires financial investment. If the designer wishes to use his or her involvement for business promotion as well as personal satisfaction, assess what advantage paid membership will gain. If it ensures invitations to openings and previews, and a listing in a brochure or annual report, then the opportunity for contacts and the good PR of supporting local culture is both worthwhile and a legitimate business expense.

Planning to take advantage of opportunities is a pro-active way of thinking that takes practice and forethought. The first and easiest activity is to have business cards and a few business brochures on hand for the casual opportunity to give them out. *Opportunities for good public relations are everywhere, but they often occur unexpectedly.*

The designer should keep informed of local news related to business. It is possible to get on many specialized mailing lists such as real estate news, government tourism activity notices, business development news (for example, through the Chamber of Commerce), cultural affairs newsletters, and so on. The designer must then take time, or appoint an employee, to scan these specialized news sources for pertinent information that will provide a source of conversation and possible follow-up for business reasons.

Excellent public relations opportunities exist with clients; the very best PR is word-of-mouth referral. In the course of professional practice, the designer should keep this in mind at all times and, as well as doing good professional work, be sure to be personally involved in final supervision. Getting to know and like clients and having them know, like, and *trust* you is the very best PR a designer can hope for.

It is pro-active thinking to encourage clients to give a reception or make an announcement at the completion of a project–good advertising for the client *and* the design firm. Provide the client with a rationale about the design for use in interviews with other client companies or the press.

Opportunities for speaking and/or writing about a specific design subject or a broad area of the built environment should be explored. Establish a connection between the subject area and the designer's expertise. In addition to "live audiences," the print medium, local radio, and television may be outlets for such general-interest pieces. Assess the medium and its audience.

The **appropriate media for designers** include
- professional interior design magazines
- professional architecture/interior design magazines
- consumer, shelter, and non-design trade magazines
- newspapers, television, radio

**Public Relations
Activity**

Determine where a talk may be given or an article submitted. Provide subject matter that will be of sufficiently broad interest to justify acceptance by the group or the paper, but which at the same time will reach a particular audience. Relevancy to current issues is vital.

If the designer does not feel comfortable as an author, identify an appropriate reporter or free-lance contributor and approach that individual to do a story. The designer will still have to prepare the basic information and be interviewed on the subject. The writer will then compose the story, quoting the designer as the authority. Local papers are always hungry for material, as indicated by the number of wire service "fillers" they use. The story should be topical and local, as well as interesting to the general public.

If the designer is not competent as a public speaker, this skill must be learned. It is an essential part of selling services.

Guidelines for Submissions

Editors of design publications will not know about a project unless the information is submitted to them. The following guidelines have been developed by editors of trade magazines for design firms who wish to submit project details for publication.

Submit a Data Sheet

Submit a data sheet or fact sheet, separate from the covering letter. This should include:

▸ design firm, name and address, and contact person's name, telephone and fax numbers
▸ project name and location
▸ date of submission
▸ completion date of the project
▸ brief profile of the project
▸ information about the personnel involved, for example, the architect, the project coordinator, the contractor, and trade resources
▸ information about the sources (wall coverings, flooring, furniture, and so on)
▸ information about the photography (who shot it? in what form? who will supply photos? who has the photography credit?)

If possible, try to keep to one page. If more pages are required, put *more* at the bottom of the first page and the project name and page number at the top left of all succeeding pages. At the end of data pages, put ### to show that no more information is forthcoming.

Submit Good Photography

Interior design photography is an art and requires a professional. However, in the initial stages of submitting work to a magazine, colored slides are adequate. These need not be professional, but the designer should ensure that they explain enough about the project so that the editor can determine if it is useable by the magazine. Professional photographers can be hired if and when it is decided to publish the project.

The best reproductions are from the original transparencies. Publishers prefer 4" x 5" format, but 35 mm, or 2$\frac{1}{4}$" x 2$\frac{1}{4}$" are acceptable.

Include a caption for each photograph.

Design professionals are not expected to be journalists–and few are. Give all pertinent information, and let the writing pros put it in article form.

Don't Try to Write for Publication

If the client has a professional PR staff or consultants, work closely with them. Compile a data sheet, offer to draft the concept and design rationale, and do anything else that may help.

Most editors require *exclusive* stories. Do not submit the same project to more than one publication at a time. When presenting material, state whether it has been submitted to other publications before or whether this is the first presentation. Keep copies of all information and photography submitted, and consider purchasing reprints of your published works for PR purposes.

Finally, designers need to deal with occasional poor PR in a positive manner. If serious difficulties arise, as they inevitably do from time to time, *act*, don't ignore; apologize, explain, and mollify. With reasonable and calm behavior, the client's annoyance will, at the very least, be minimized. If a real crisis generates adverse publicity, a statement clearly explaining the situation should be prepared. In the course of work, keep in mind the degree of responsibility and liability a designer must bear and the effect of one negative situation on future business.

Dealing with Problems

Promotion is necessary for one important reason–the designer's livelihood. *No project* equals *no income*, and projects rarely find the designer; the designer must seek them out. Young professionals in all fields have to start somewhere; promotional activities evolve as the designer gains experience. First projects are a challenge to obtain, but each successful project makes promotion for, and acquisition of, the next job easier.

Promotion

Promotional Goals

The firm's overall goals and objectives are the motivating force behind promotional activity. Goals address the designer's or firm's objectives in terms of professional development, achievement, satisfaction, finances, and organization. Both long-term and short-term goals should be reviewed annually.

Goal-setting is undertaken in a meeting, or series of meetings, by the principals of the firm and others as required, with time to think and discuss without interruption. In an established firm, goal-setting accompanies a review of the past year's accomplishments. In a beginning firm, goals are based on realistic hopes and aspirations about the firm's future. Open-ended questions are posed to elicit thought and discussion: "Where would we like to be in terms of our professional development next year? in five years? What would we like to achieve? Are we happy with our work? Is the profit margin sufficient? Does the office run efficiently? Is the staff overworked? Do we need more or less personnel?" Thoughtful answers will result in the firm's long-term goals.

Short-term objective-setting takes place with long-term goals clearly in mind and written down. These objectives are set in a time-frame of a year or less, and spell out exactly what is to be achieved, how it is to be done, by whom, with what resources, and by what date. They should also include "what if" scenarios and contingency plans to correct any malfunctions. During formation of the short-term objectives, one may affect another and force adjustment.

The bottom line of all business goals and objectives is the financial health of the firm. Long-term goals may include consolidating the firm's position in a particular specialty if work in that area is both satisfactory and profitable, or they may include phasing out of a certain area and attempting to enter new areas, or a combination of both.

Whatever the long-term design direction, the firm's current and near-future projects must be sufficient in number and profitability to allow continuance and growth. Promotional activity must therefore both reflect the firm's overall future goals and enable them to be realized. As an example, a small firm doing mainly residential

---

Guidelines for Public Relations Self-Evaluation

Image-building public relations activities are vital to a design firm's marketing strategy. The following questions should stimulate thinking and help create positive responses.

- Is the office well designed?
- Does someone in the firm have specific responsibility for supervising and maintaining a public relations program?
- Are any editors of design publications, business or building editors of newspapers, or editors of community papers known personally by someone in the firm?
- When the interior design for a new building has been accepted, does the firm send photographs or copy to the newspapers?
- Has anyone in the firm given a speech before a community group within the past three months?
- Does the firm submit project information to design publications?
- When the firm has the contract for a bank, large office, school, or other building of specialized interest, is information regarding the project offered to trade magazines serving that field?
- Does the firm have a brochure to distribute to prospective clients?
- Does the firm maintain a file of slides of its best projects for presentation to public groups and prospective clients?
- Do the principals of the firm belong to community, civic, or service groups?
- Is anyone in the firm personally acquainted with people of influence within the municipal government? within the provincial or state governments? with federal representatives?
- Does the firm support the public relations program of the professional association?
- When new partners, associates, or project heads are appointed or promoted, is the announcement sent to the newspapers' business pages or city editors or both?
- Does the firm have an established system for informing employees of the firm's position on community matters or how it serves the community?
- Does the firm handle all prospective clients courteously, even when their project is not of interest?
- When they are developing publicity for a project, is assistance offered to building owners, realtors, and builders with whom the firm deals?
- Is anyone in the firm available to the professional association for career counseling services for the school system, the post-secondary educational system, or vocational guidance programs?
- Is the firm familiar with the policies and activities of the professional association?

work may have a long-term goal to move into corporate and commercial work. It would be foolhardy to put *all* the promotional dollars and effort into attracting corporate clients. New residential work will need to be brought in to provide the ongoing cash flow.

Exactly what to promote requires careful self-assessment, the ability to accurately outline the scope of services offered, and a willingness to admit constraints.

It is necessary, of course, to have made all basic decisions regarding the business–fees, billing procedures, and so on. It is also necessary to know the capabilities of the available support staff, sources of supply and labor, time available for new work, and the present or potential specialties of the design principal(s). As well, the designer must know the competition and the business climate and any peculiarities of the designated geographic area.

The scope of services the designer is able to provide must be outlined in detail. These must be realistic–based on the ability to handle particular projects. From the wide range of skills required for success in the field, the designer's strengths and weaknesses should be honestly assessed. Promotion should be based mainly on the firm's most competent area and secondarily on other areas where expertise is growing. The promotional material must outline carefully, and in detail, the range of services offered.

Constraints should be assessed so that the firm does not promote services it is not equipped to handle. Constraints may be based on time or the availability of competent sub-contractors. It is essential that whatever business the promotion attracts can be carried out efficiently.

Promotional Content

As promotion is an advertisement of the design firm's professional services, tangible evidence of what is being offered should be available. This may take various forms–including the "tools" mentioned on pages 64 and 65, the business card and brochure.

A personal letter of introduction is an effective and low-cost way of promoting the designer or design firm. This must be brief and well written, outlining the designer's (or firm's) capabilities and experience, and highlighting any special features.

The designer's or design firm's portfolio or a well-produced series of slides or a video may be shown to specific audiences. A useful tool is a mini-portfolio. It consists of a brief resumé, a selected number of photographs, colored photocopies of drawings or sketches, all of a size that can be duplicated in quantity and easily mailed. The portfolio can be as inexpensive or expensive as you wish. At a visual event, there must be something for people to take away with them, in most cases the company's brochure.

The design firm may introduce itself to potential clients by presenting a gift such as a paperweight or well-designed calendar, along with a letter outlining the design firm's expertise and interest in the prospect's type of environment.

Paid advertisements are very expensive and may also violate ethical standards in the locale of practice. An exception may be ads in smaller media (symphony programs, art gallery newsletters, and so on) with select audiences.

Direct Promotion

Indirect Promotion

Indirect promotion may be defined as that situation where a third party (or more) comes between the design firm and the intended audience. While indirect promotion usually originates with the firm, it is not as controllable as, for instance, mailing a letter and brochure to a prospective client. Examples are media releases, articles or stories about the firm or its work, design competitions or exhibits sponsored by others.

Media releases must be simple and straightforward; observe the W5H rule–who, what, where, when, why, and how. Use plain language in short, clear sentences that tell the news briefly; one page should be sufficient. Devise a short, interest-generating first sentence. Phrases such as "wish to announce" are outmoded; simply state what it is that is being announced. Be sure all names are spelled correctly, all initials and titles are right. Do not editorialize; opinions are not news.

The content of a release must be newsworthy to the media. From the designer's or firm's viewpoint, it must advertise and promote. The challenge is to balance these two aims in such a way that editors or news managers do not feel they are being used for free advertising. Make sure that the news is legitimately interesting to the medium's audience.

Articles about the designer or firm may be authored by the designer and submitted to the media, or the designer may work through a professional writer (usually associated with a PR firm) who uses the designer's notes to compose an interesting, well-written story. The daily or weekly newspaper, general-interest or professional magazine or journal should be carefully selected. This requires familiarity with their content, format, features, publication schedule, and policy on unsolicited manuscripts. Information on the latter two may be obtained from the publication's masthead, usually located within the first few pages, which lists the publisher, editor, and so forth. While the articles for public relations purposes referred to earlier are general in content, articles for promotional purposes focus on the expertise, capabilities, or achievements of the designers or firm in such a way as to generate the public's interest in obtaining their professional services. (Of course any article published actually serves both functions.) Refer to the *Guidelines for Submission* on page 70.

Photographs are essential and must be of professional quality. They may be submitted by the designer or it may be noted on the release that the clients have agreed to have photographs taken.

The content must be concise, to the point, and cover all details. A good lead sentence and first paragraph are

---

How to Prepare a Media Release

▶ 1. Use white 8 ¹/₂" x 11" standard paper–not legal size, half length, or other odd shapes.

▶ 2. Use only one side of the paper. When using more than one sheet, clip them together, do not staple them.

▶ 3. Place the source of the news release in the upper left-hand corner of each page. Give the contact's name, the name of the firm, address, and telephone and fax numbers. Unless the source is declared on the copy, the release will probably not be used. Make sure the contact named is reachable by phone or fax.

▶ 4. Locate the release date in the upper right-hand corner. Normally state "for immediate release"; if the subject is not time-sensitive, state "for release at will" or "use at will."

▶ 5. Good quality photocopies are essential. If the release is sent to one medium representative only, state "exclusive."

▶ 6. No title is necessary. Editors prefer to write the headlines.

▶ 7. Allow ample margins–at least one inch on each side and two to three inches at the top–for the editor to write notes and heads.

▶ 8. Double-space the copy. This makes it easier to read and edit.

▶ 9. Fold the release so that the copy shows *outside*. Outward folding facilitates getting to the copy immediately.

reading of the whole article.

A final note: A professional writer can make the difference between acceptance and rejection of an article. Give the writer ideas and let him or her sell the story with professional writing skills. (As mentioned earlier, this kind of writer will usually be associated with a PR firm.)

Design competitions are a fine source of promotion. Before entering, check to ensure that entries will be on display and–if so, where. Then, whether or not the project submitted is a winner, the public will get to view the work. Winning or placing in a design competition has additional value because the award can be mentioned in all promotional material.

Competition entries of actual work require the clients' permission. Check whether you may divulge their addresses and the costs of the projects. It is recommended that such permissions be obtained in writing.

Personal Contact

In the end, the selling of design services depends on personal contact. Whether the personal contact is generated through promotion, referral, personal search, or a formal proposal request, the sale can only be made through person-to-person communication.

To sell professional design services is to convince a prospective client that a required end product will be delivered satisfactorily. Put another way, the client buys a *vision* of a finished project; the designer sells a *promise* to make the vision real. Services are intangible; realizing this restriction focuses the designer's attention on the necessity to emphasize the end-product benefits to the client.

> **Selling design services involves**
> ▸ **finding the client**
> ▸ **interesting the client**
> ▸ **motivating the client**

Statistically–as determined through questionnaires and tabulation by professional organizations–most design business (40 to 50 percent) is generated through personal (or firm) search and subsequent "cold calls," another 20 to 25 percent of work comes through referrals from past clients, and roughly the same percentage emanates as new work from former clients.

Finding the Client

There is no magic formula for this task. Public relations activities and promotion identify contacts: individuals who are in a position to personally use interior design services, who are in businesses that may need interior design, or who know an individual or firm who may be sold on the value of professional assistance. Being alert and attentive to opportunities is perhaps the best business faculty to cultivate.

Interesting the Client

Before attempting to sell services directly, the designer must find out as much as possible about the prospective client. Any approach must be based on information and analysis, and then scaled to the needs of the individuals involved.

A prospective client may either own or rent premises, but the owner of the property is always involved, and often pays for or shares in the cost of leasehold improvements. The design firm will have to put promotional tools to work that will attract the attention of such prospects.

Motivating the Client

Designers with interested prospective clients must demonstrate the benefits of interior design. Stress aspects that are of real importance to the clients. Often, several individuals make up the client group, particularly when building owners are different individuals or firms than the users. There must be a harmonious relationship between the owner's interest in a building, the users' wants and needs, and the designer's ability to provide the necessary services.

Implementing the Plan of Action

In order to successfully practice interior design and market professional services, a design firm must know its capabilities and must have set goals consistent with these capabilities. Limitations must also be assessed and the prospective work must meet these criteria. The business plan evolves from this overall self-assessment. Business direction, like the goal-setting mentioned earlier, changes and grows with the firm; it is particularly important for new professionals to set realistic targets for a one- or two-year period. Long-range goals, five or ten years distant, will direct the shorter-range goals and the yearly objectives.

Because referrals from, and other work for, the same client are an important source of new projects, it is essential to "keep on top and keep in touch" after the initial contact. Any work undertaken must be done well, but for future business it must also be *seen* to be done well. Designers should supervise closely, inspect thoroughly, and celebrate each project's completion with the clients.

On any referral work, follow through with the marketing plan as soon as possible. Potential clients are impressed–and hopefully secured–with such things as brochures, promotional packages, proposals, that reach them quickly; this demonstrates genuine interest, efficiency, and good business.

Prospect Contact Report

The prospect contact report (see figure 2) is a confidential office document that records information on each prospective client and the design firm's comments and assessments.

Checklist

▸ prospect's name
▸ date and method of initial contact (phone/letter/personal contact, request for proposal)
▸ contact's name: correct spelling, initials, title (if possible, include name of person within the contact's firm who makes decisions)
▸ correct address of prospect including company name and department, postal code, phone and fax numbers
▸ type of business
▸ nature of current project requirement(s)
    facilities study
    feasibility study
    planning
    interior design
    furniture selection/design
▸ approximate cost of project (guesstimate round figures, such as $10,000, $100,000, or $1,000,000)
▸ approximate size of project in square feet/square meters
▸ date client wants construction to start
▸ other designers being considered
▸ date formal interview scheduled and where

▸ information source for this project
▸ date selection to be made

The following data should also be recorded:

▸ the prospect initiation: by previous client? by close acquaintance? from publication? from third party? through firm's reputation? from a "cold" call?
▸ prospective client status: current client (non-related project), current client (related project), previous client, or new prospect
▸ prospect status:

speculative–not defined
defined, but over a year away
defined, less than a year away
invited to interview
interviewed (five or more firms)
interviewed, short list

▸ significant events and dates:

letter of interest due
interview scheduled
proposal requested
expected contract award date
other (explain)

▸ contacts since last update: calls made, calls received, correspondence, visits to or visits by
▸ reminders: who and when to call or write or visit (transfer to daily calendar)
▸ general comments or thoughts: regarding project and/or prospect firm and/or individuals
▸ form completed by: name and date

A separate master list of prospects documents *all* contacts and also serves as the index to the contact reports. On this master list, the date of contact, by whom, firm name, nature of possible work, contact report (yes/no), and date to recontact are the only items recorded. Following the award of each contract for design services, a letter expressing thanks or disappointment should be sent to the prospect.

Selling Design Means Selling the Designer

Selling design often includes "selling" the designer(s) as well as the design services and solutions. Selling the designer or, more accurately, communicating the designer's personality and style is accomplished through good public relations activity and through being consistently professional in business dealings. Develop and project honesty, reliability, and enthusiasm for interior design at all times.

Selling design services involves convincing prospective clients of professional capabilities and expertise so that they are comfortable in giving the designer both their confidence and their promise to pay for the services.

Presentations

7

Presentations are pre-packaged sales tools prepared in advance to suit particular prospects, and delivered both orally and with visual and printed support material.

Any presentation may be a solo performance by one design company or one of two-to-five appearances by competing firms before the same potential client. Do not be concerned about where you fall in the presentation line-up; concentrate on developing the best presentation possible.

Determine the purpose of the presentation and review the following selling principles:

▶ Give the buyer a choice between something and something– never between something and nothing.
▶ Don't ask "if," ask "which."
▶ Learn the client's/users' viewpoint and adapt to it.
▶ Remember that the important points are those that are of most interest to the clients/users, not the designer.
▶ Be honest and straightforward.
▶ Repeat the message–the more it is repeated in different ways the more it will be believed.
▶ Use factual evidence to support your case: project histories, experience with related projects, and so on.
▶ Care about the client/users in order to proceed with conviction.
▶ Be prepared: if you know the information, a more positive, assertive, and confident image will be projected.
▶ Have the package prepared well in advance in order to have an opportunity to rehearse.
▶ Develop a unified graphic look around the selling theme: a look of quality that is distinctive and attention-getting.

Principles of Selling

The research and analysis of the client's background and needs, along with the detailed self-analysis of the firm's capabilities, will form the basis for the content of the presentation.

The package
▶ the written, graphic, and visual material to be left with the client
▶ the visual materials to be used in the presentation
▶ the notes of the oral presentation

The presenters
▶ most effectively, two to four persons

The event, which may be
▶ a general presentation of the design capabilities of a designer or firm to a potential client
▶ more often, a presentation of a concept of, and/or solution to, a specific design project for a client's/user's review and approval

Three Main Elements of a Presentation

The Package

The presentation consists of a package of written, visual, and oral material. The *written material* is the main content of the presentation, but by its style and form it also conveys the overall organization and competence of the firm.

Written material must

▶ have a title page, a contents page, and an extremely well-organized text
▶ be written in a straightforward, concise, and easy-to-read style
▶ be neat and clean
▶ be perfect: no grammatical errors, no typos, no misspellings
▶ (For greater detail, see *Proposal Guidelines*, page 64.)

Visual material is either included as part of the written material or used as a visual aid to the oral presentation. Within the package, visuals may consist of charts, graphs, detailed sketches, plans, photographs, and so on. Visuals contained within the written material should follow the established format. In addition, they must be well executed and neatly and legibly labeled.

Visual material used to illustrate and demonstrate the design firm's capabilities and experience, or used in conjunction with particular points in the oral presentation, must first be clear to the audience. Whether the material is on a flip chart, presentation boards, slides, video, or film, it must have labeling that can be read by all, and the image must be as clear and concise as possible.

All visuals, particularly graphs, should have an integrated look.

Oral material starts with a well-researched, well-developed outline. *Exactly* what is going to be said, and by whom, must be written down in an orderly fashion (a script), checked for content, checked against the written material, checked against the visual aids, edited to be totally clear, using straightforward language understandable to the prospective audience, and then rehearsed by the participants at least once.

Depending upon the presenters, this *script* may be read with pauses for elaboration, questions, or references to the visual aids. These pauses, of course, must be estimated as to time required, keyed to, and rehearsed with, the script. Alternately, the presenter may feel comfortable with notes only, but these should be well ordered and sufficiently detailed to prevent inadvertently leaving something out.

Consider that an audience remembers only 20 percent of what is heard and 30 percent of what is seen.

Presentation Methods (in order of preference)

▶ Outline method–involves preparation of presentation outline, sequence of visual aids, oral presentation notes, and so on (highly recommended)
▶ Memorization method–text is written out, then committed to memory (often the presenter concentrates so hard on remembering the correct words and sequence that the presentation sounds stilted, the point of the presentation is lost, and the audience is turned off)
▶ Manuscript method–text is written out and delivered word-for-word (can be dull and lacks eye contact)
▶ Impromptu ad-lib method (not recommended)

Communication Points Checklist

The following section is a checklist of communication points to be considered by the interior designer developing the oral material.

Audience Analysis

▶ Who will be listening to the presentation?
▶ What does the audience *want* to know?
▶ What does the audience *need* to know?

▸ What is the size of the audience versus the number of
presenters and the type of visual aids?

▸ How can the designer ensure the audience's attention?
▸ Which attention factors might be included?
    activity   familiarity   conflict   movement   novelty
    humor   reality   suspense   vital information
    health and security

Attention Factors

▸ How will the design solution benefit the client and users?
Tangible benefits might include
    reasonable cost
    decreased absenteeism
    less employee turn-over, happier employees, more
      productive employees
    opportunity to impress the client's clients
    increased business
    more efficient production
    better health, safety, welfare
    less maintenance
    security

**Motivation
Development**

    A *presentation outline* is prepared in advance as a blue-
print to the upcoming event. The presentation outline states
▸ what is to be included in the presentation, in detail
▸ the terms and sequence in which the design concept will be
presented
▸ how visual aids, question-and-answer periods, and breaks are
to be scheduled within the presentation time frame
▸ a review of pertinent information from previous presentations

The Presentation

Outline

    The presentation has four main components:
▸ the introduction: a strong opening statement that catches
attention and establishes the tone of the presentation
▸ the central idea: an explanation of the design concept or
main point of the presentation, in terms relevant to the idea
being presented
▸ the main body of information, which should
    detail the *what* of the design solution
    explain the *why* of the design solution
    contain well-reasoned logic focused at the audience
    reinforce the design decisions by referring to the
      research results, that is, the *programming* of the
      project
    support and justify the design decisions using statistics,
      specific instances, testimonies, and analogies
    provide information that assists the client in making a
      decision (consider giving the client a choice between
      design solutions by discussing the advantages and
      disadvantages of each)
    use human-interest stories, if relevant, to illustrate a
      point
    include other necessary information, such as an
      explanation of the design process, or an explanation of
      the progress of a project
▸ the conclusion, which states
    brief summaries of major points
    indication to the audience of the response and action
      expected of them
    a strong closing message

Contents

Schedule

▸ What is to be discussed in the presentation? In what terms, and in what sequence?
▸ When planning the presentation, consider
chronological order
spatial relationships
cause-and-effect relationships
statement of problem and solution
comparisons of pros and cons, advantages and
disadvantages

> To be seen as efficient and effective, nothing is a substitute for knowing the material thoroughly.

▸ For relevancy and emphasis, how will the visual aids be scheduled within the time-frame? Will breaks be scheduled? of what duration? As attention span is usually fifty to fifty-five minutes; scheduled visuals, question-and-answer periods, and breaks can be of valuable assistance in changing the pace, refreshing the audience, and so on.
▸ On what date will the presentation outline be complete? Is there time to check for completeness?
▸ At the presentation review and rehearsal, briefly discuss style of dress, coordination between the presenters, and so on. Each presenter may then attend to these personal details so that they do not become an issue immediately before the presentation.
▸ Following the presentation, file the outline (usually in point form) in the client's folder for future reference.

The Presenters

The presenters should be familiar with
▸ the design firm's capabilities
▸ the design firm's history, background, and principals
▸ the prospective client's scope of business (if applicable), premises, and principals
▸ the client's needs
▸ present and future possibilities
▸ individual idiosyncrasies of the project (if applicable)
▸ the presentation package and all visual aids
▸ the project at hand (if applicable)

Speaking in public, even to small groups, is a fearful prospect for many people. Without some training and opportunities to practice, designers who are nervous and unsure of their personal capability in this area will be unable to convey the confidence necessary to sell design services. To become comfortable and skilled at speaking, it is worthwhile for both design firms and individuals to avail themselves of professional help. It is certainly possible to learn this talent and well worth the effort needed to do so. Communication and media experts may be contacted in all major cities; their expertise and their use of closed-circuit TV for teaching purposes will be of great help to inexperienced speakers.

For rehearsal of a particular presentation, firms may wish to consider renting (or buying, if long-term use is foreseen) a video camera to film and then review the performances of the presenters. So much of a communication's impact is conveyed by means of voice, tone, expression, and gesture that it is definitely an asset to have the presenters aware of their strengths and weaknesses in this area. When preparing for a presentation

- Be neat and well groomed.
- Project a serious business image, avoiding extremes of fashion.
- Be true to your own personal style.
- Be attired appropriately to the time of day, season, and other circumstances, to avoid distracting the audience.

Appearance, the First Impression

- Use a clear, confident voice, loud enough to be heard.
- Avoid a lecture tone. Speak *to* the clients, not *at* them. Avoid design jargon which would be beyond the average layman's understanding.
- Modulate: vary the voice to express enthusiasm, sincerity, confidence.
- Vary the pitch, pace, and volume for emphasis.
- Articulate the words.

Voice

- Use precise vocabulary; there are *right* words for everything!
- Use correct grammar.
- Avoid slang, clichés, and colloquialisms.

Language

- Don't forget the warmth of a genuine smile.
- Take the initiative with handshaking.
- Don't slouch or fumble with your hands.
- Don't chew gum, your lips, cheeks, pen, hair, or fingernails!
- Maintain frequent eye-contact with each member of the audience. (If you are reading a script, this is difficult but not impossible.)
- Relax, and enjoy the event!

Body Language

With everything prepared–the package, the visuals, the script, the presenters–allot enough time to double-check material and equipment. In general, planning for the unexpected usually assures that every possible contingency is covered. Know where the presentation is to take place, how to get there and how long it takes, and where to park. Or book a taxi in advance. The presentation must not be late, and time must be allowed for set up.

In advance of the day, the host/prospect should be made aware of how many people are in the presentation party. (The prospect has to prepare, too.) Find out, as well, the size of the audience in order to establish the size of the presentation team.

The Presentation Event

Determine the time alloted for the presentation and consider the following details:
- dimensions and shape of the room
- location of all entrances
- windows: exposure and blinds (darkened room necessary)
- arrangement of furnishings: shape of the set-up (boardroom, theater, classroom, horseshoe)
- electrical outlets: location, type of plug required
- location of lights and light switches

Consider the Physical Environment

▸ acoustics: is a microphone necessary? (check floor coverings, ceilings, wall hangings; talk and listen from various parts of the room)

▸ lectern: is one available? is it set to the right height? is there lighting for the lectern?

▸ availability of other equipment: whiteboard/chalkboard, flip-chart and easel, pin-up wall surface, display rail; chalk, erasers, felt-tip pens, and a pointer

▸ electrical equipment: is a table or regular projection stand available for projection equipment? are screens available? if you are using an overhead projector, does the screen have a keystone eliminator arm? can the audience view the screen well?

▸ pre-presentation availability: when can equipment be set up? will help be available?

▸ all audio/visual equipment (such as slide projectors, video equipment) and materials: inspect everything that is to be used in the presentation: check extension cords, plug adapters, remote control cords, dissolve units, spare fuses, and extra projection lamps; include a flashlight, and tweezers for stuck slides

General Presentation of Design Capabilities

The research and analysis of the client's background, concerns, and needs, along with the detailed self-analysis of the design firm's capabilities, dictates the content of a presentation. The intent of the presentation is to show how interior design can help, and specifically how this particular interior designer or firm can be of service. Whether the design firm is seeking work from a particular prospect or wooing a client, it is important to determine and develop the sales theme utilizing all available resources.

Presentation of a Concept/Solution to the Client

Knowledge of the client's/users' needs and concerns assists in developing the approach necessary for presentations made during the programming stage, the design concept stage, and during design development.

The guidelines should be reviewed. Remember that an important part of the presentation at the conceptual stage is the participation of the client and/or committee members.

Encouraging Client Participation

Questions and answers   Planning for question-and-answer periods is an easy way to ensure audience involvement.

▸ Listen to questions carefully; they indicate whether or not the presentation has been understood. (Questions may indirectly voice objections to the design solution.)

▸ Answer questions carefully after first making sure everyone has heard them; avoid sounding defensive.

▸ Be prepared for the question-and-answer period; if necessary, prepare a list of possible questions with their answers.

▸ Use the question-and-answer period to drive home important points one more time.

Other techniques   There are several techniques that ensure participation in a discussion–asking direct questions, for instance, or asking for opinions. Other methods may include brainstorming; group discussions; questionnaires; a vote between choices; and physical involvement with actual samples such as textiles, furnishings, lighting.

Remember that the client is a member of the design team. Reinforce the fact that it is the *client's* project, not the designer's. Avoid pronouns that give the impression that it is *your* project. In general, avoid overuse of personal pronouns, which can be confusing.

Evaluation

Designers should evaluate all presentations for their own future reference. Explore what could have been done better, with more refinement, more "polish."

A presentation–including the written, graphic, and visual materials; the event; and the presenters–should leave all or most of the following impressions with the prospective client:

A Good Presentation Makes Good Impressions

► That the firm approaches a project considering all of the owner's concerns, functional and operational needs, costs, and occupancy schedule–as well as design and general appearance.
► That the firm's actual experience proves its ability to plan and design facilities that will fully serve the owner's functional and operational purposes, and that the firm is a leader in these areas.
► That the firm's actual experience proves its ability to plan and design the facility to be built to meet the occupancy schedule.
► That the firm's experience proves its ability to apply its design capabilities creatively to meet the practical requirements of function, cost, and schedule, and still produce an attractive whole.
► That the firm can deal effectively with the many management problems (community relations, difficult contractors, and so on) that will undoubtedly occur during the development of the project.
► That the firm will give full consideration to the thoughts and ideas of the owners(s).
► That the firm's reputation with its clients will assure the client a productive and harmonious association.
► That the firm has the capacity and capabilities needed to complete the project.
► That senior, highly qualified personnel will give their full attention to the project because it is important to them.
► That the firm has already demonstrated its understanding of the problems (needs) to be solved in order to achieve the owner's goals and objectives.
► That the firm's actual experience proves its ability to deal creatively with the objective of obtaining maximum operational and functional advantages within the budgeted cost.

Presentation Guidelines

► Develop rapport with the audience.
► Set the tone for presentation; let the audience unwind from other activities and relax before beginning.
► Introduce members of the team to audience members.
► Briefly review the client's needs and, from previous discussion, what the client thinks the designer might be able to provide.
► Cover all information pertinent to the prospect's interests: who the designer is, what the designer can do for the client, how it is done, how the designer's experience relates to the client, how the services will benefit the client.
► Frequently emphasize and restate interest in the client's project.
► Be brief and to the point in all aspects of the presentation.
► Summarize the presentation, reminding the audience of all important points.
► Thank the prospect for the opportunity to present.
► Follow up with either a proposal that is left with the client or a letter summarizing all the major points covered in the presentation.
► Organize a tour of the design firm's premises so the prospect can see the operation firsthand.
► Organize tours of completed projects.

Summary

Depending on market, competition, and successful promotion, it takes perhaps fifty calls to acquire one client. There are no guarantees. Decision-making processes may depend upon the political situation; what "connections"– personal or political–are at work; or evaluation in comparison to other projects, clients, designers. Occasionally, who is going to get the contract has been predetermined. Sometimes it is a matter of timing.

Whatever the reason for getting or *not* getting a job, the final test of a true professional is *discretion*. Clients, prospective clients, and other professionals must always be treated with respect, regardless of the decision.

According to surveys, clients evaluating interior design firms found that the following factors had the most influence on their decisions (listed in order of importance):

1. Professional experience
► track record of project experience
► expertise specifically related to the project under consideration
2. Cost performance
► delivery of project on budget
3. Schedule performance
► plans and specifications
► construction/implementation
► follow-up
4. Design excellence
► general reputation
► reputation specific to project type
► ability to interpret client's requirements
► ability to balance function, solution, economics, and aesthetics
► concern for life safety and welfare
► ability to solve problems with original ideas
5. Effective relationships
► with clients on other projects
► with contractors
► with municipal, provincial, state, federal authorities
6. Genuine interest in the project
7. Salesmanship
► effective performance
8. Price
9. Design originality
► ability to develop an efficient and economical aesthetic solution
10. Integrity
11. Available resources
► financial
► personnel
► appropriate expertise, either internal or external
12. Supervision
► proximity of firm to job site
► meeting client's expectations

Project Management

Planning and Preparation

Preparing for work on an interior design project entails a period of assessment, allocation of resources, team planning, and the set-up of a filing and documentation system.

The scope of the work and its impact on the firm will already have been assessed, but actually obtaining the contract necessitates a closer examination of all the project's ramifications.

A file number should be assigned to the project as a first step toward organization. This number is used as an identifier on *all* paperwork: plans, files, correspondence, reports, budgets, tenders, purchase orders, invoices, and payments made and received.

Resources to be allocated include personnel, space, supplies, and time. These items will have been discussed previously; at this stage they are refined.

Planning involves everyone on the creative design team. The team discusses task allocation, specific consultants needed, and any other outside participation. A project meeting schedule may be drawn up, the site discussed in general terms, and particular information shared. This early organizational discussion builds rapport within the team who will be creating and implementing the design project.

All contents of the project file should be identified with the file number assigned to the project.

The Project File

The project file includes
- the contract–a photocopy of the signed contract, which can be highlighted or marked as required for reference throughout the project
- personnel–all pertinent names, addresses, phone and fax numbers, and positions of the following:
    client
    owner (if different than the client)
    client contact
    consultants
    team members (this file will grow as the project
      progresses and be well used by the team)
- budgets–this section may need to be subdivided as the project progresses; it may also contain photocopies of team members' time sheets
- critical path–the critical path document is not an item to be filed, but a copy in the file is useful for reference and will keep track of changes in scheduling
- correspondence–general
- tenders–tender documents, addenda, contracts, purchase orders
- reports–meeting reports with clients, planning meeting notes, site visit reports, and others
- proposed change notices
- change orders–if executed
- payments–certificates for payment

Depending on the level of computerization in the design firm, some of the above information may be recorded in a computerized job file. Unless all team members have access to and operate work stations, it is recommended that the hands-on files be maintained.

A final note: Never put an undated piece of paper in a file, and avoid the strictly numerical form of dating: 6/3 will be March 6 to one person and June 3 to another.

Communication Reports

The communication report is a multipurpose form for recording specific information concerning any phase of a project. It is used

- for memos
- to record telephone conversations
- to summarize meetings
- to record specific decisions

A communication report is issued by the designer directly to all parties involved in, or affected by, the contents. The communication report (figure 3) may be used as a model. The report should include the following:

- design firm logo, name, address, telephone and fax numbers
- title of the form: *Communication Report* (or similar name)
- project name and address
- file number
- date
- name and address of person to receive the communication
- name of person sending the communication
- names and companies of participants engaged in the telephone call or meeting
- indication of how the communication took place
- information to be recorded
- list of persons to receive copies
- signature
- cautionary note, such as: *If there are any discrepancies in the above, please notify the writer immediately, otherwise the contents of the report will be considered acceptable to all.*

The Critical Path

A critical path is a scheduling tool. It is a projected plan of activity, leading to the fulfillment of a particular goal. It is a graphic presentation of a horizontal time line on which the interrelationships of parts can be viewed and the milestones noted. It is one document detailing the activity schedules of many parties over a period of time.

A critical path might include:

- project name, file number, name of designer
- signing date of contract

outline of the scope of services as listed in the contract for the project (but including more detailed information) divided into stages, with a time frame indicated for each stage.

Critical paths are not cast in stone, but because *time* is the vital ingredient in the design service being sold, the preparation of the critical path is worthy of the team's serious consideration and best efforts. Critical paths are used in-house and are also distributed to the client, consultants, and contractors. When determining a critical path, designers must be particularly careful as it is a commitment to complete phases of the project by particular dates, and clients consider scheduling (time) and budgeting (money) to be the two most important aspects of interior design services.

The work schedule is based on the firm's past experience, staff allocations, the nature of the work, and the agreed-upon time span of the contract. A reasonable schedule produces efficient work. People seem to work best when they know their time allotments for various tasks. In general, deadlines produce results.

The critical path document synthesizes the work requirements, the stages of the design project, and the time frame into a comprehensible whole.

Format of a Critical Path

A critical path will, first of all, be a visual representation of the time available for the project, starting with the contract date and ending at the projected completion date. Particular design and implementation tasks are listed and the time line is divided into segments (weeks, months). The project's tasks are then plotted on the time line. *Milestones* or *checkpoints*–deadlines for completion of certain phases, for presentations to clients for approval, and so on–are added and accentuated for easy reference. These can be identified by numbers keyed to a written list located below the time line.

The critical path is, as noted, a scheduling tool. In order to use it to the best advantage, regular critical-path reviews by the design team must be scheduled, with adjustments made as required.

The critical path notes the main stages of the project, that is: programming, design concept, design development, contract documentation, contract administration, and evaluation. Further specification of particular tasks is a matter of choice. One solution for a complex program is to plot the critical path of the "whole picture," and then excerpt either short time periods or specific tasks and plot them separately. In either case, the whole-picture critical path must be updated and reviewed on a regular basis.

Content of a Critical Path

Critical paths are excellent tools and familiarity with them adds a good measure of easily assimilated organization to the designer's work.

**Stages of
the Project**

The stages of a project flow forward, with varying degrees of overlap, in the following order:
▸programming
▸design concept
▸design development
▸contract documentation
▸contract administration
▸evaluation

Programming

Writing the design program is clarifying, to the satisfaction of both the client and the designer, exactly what is needed and wanted in the space under consideration, giving the rationale for each point. It is a lengthy investigative process, sometimes taking up to one-third of the project's total time.

Programming is a pre-design stage which occurs once the contract for professional service has been signed. It is the analysis stage so necessary to the implementation of the professional interior designer's skills.

The program is usually presented to the client in two stages: first, the analysis of needs, and second, initial space planning and budgets.

Programming is discussed in greater detail in the following chapter.

In brief, during the program stage, the design firm
▸identifies and analyzes client's and users' needs and goals
▸evaluates existing premises including space allocation, furnishings and equipment, and other attributes of the existing environment
▸assesses project resources and limitations, physical and financial
▸identifies life safety and code requirements
▸considers site concerns, such as location, access, and so on
▸prepares schedule for development of the project
▸develops budgets for interior construction and furnishings
▸analyzes design objectives and spatial requirements
▸develops preliminary space planning and furniture layout
▸integrates findings with knowledge of interior design
▸determines the need for, and coordinates with, consultants and other specialists
▸investigates requirements for regulatory approval
▸organizes information for client discussion and approval

Design Concept

Following the investigation and analysis carried out in the programming stage, the designer develops concepts and makes preliminary space plans, furniture layouts, and so on.

During the conceptual design stage, the interior designer
▸formulates preliminary plans and three-dimensional design concepts that are appropriate to the program's budget and that reflect the character, function, and aesthetic of the project
▸prepares image boards
▸presents the conceptual design and preliminary cost
▸delivers estimates to the client for discussion and approval

The client's written approval must be obtained before proceeding, either through an exchange of formal letters, or through a communication report which is sent to the client with a request for a signature indicating agreement.

An interior design concept is not valid unless it is conceived in relationship to the program requirements and the space in which the interior will occur–whether it is reuse of existing space or not-yet-built new space. The aim should be to create the perfect space, but it must be within the limitations of the program and the building plans. Concepts for interior spaces are engendered by external human needs. Artists may exemplify their inner emotional needs through the design of their art pieces, but interior designers are required to turn the users' needs into tangible form, through the process of conceptual thinking.

Conceptual thinking is a process; it is thinking through the problem, considering all the ramifications of the needs expressed in the program in conjunction with the limitations of the structure and form of the physical entity. Each project has particular problems which need to be solved. A mature design solution is one which arises from a well-considered concept, one which enhances the program. If this is achieved and the solution is also unique, a great design will have been created. If, on the other hand, the solution is different only for the sake of being different and does not solve the problem in a responsive way, then the concept and solution are both less than desirable.

A concept may begin with words: a brief description of a space may engender visual thoughts. For example, the words "entry/reception area" may suggest

Initiating Conceptual Thought

▸ a strong sense of entry, definition as a separate place between where one has been and where one is going, or
▸ a strong image of the occupant of the premises, implying tradition, or forward thinking, or whatever image the client or corporation wants expressed

Translating words into visual form begins the spatial conceptualization of the program requirements.

Drawings

are graphic presentations that
- ▸ define the quantity of the space
- ▸ show size and structure
- ▸ show generic materials
- ▸ show components
- ▸ show spatial relationships

Schedules

are abbreviated notes that
- ▸ simplify by breaking into smaller parts
- ▸ deal with components
- ▸ clarify particular finishes and colors
- ▸ clarify dimensions
- ▸ clarify furnishings, fixtures, and
  materials on a component basis

Specifications

are the written text, the ultimate authority for
- ▸ physical requirements
- ▸ installation methods
- ▸ standards of workmanship
- ▸ quality of finishes, materials,
  furnishings, and fixtures
- ▸ specific warranty requirements

The concept may start with a dominant theme, such as a shape, form, color, or material, which leads into the character of the space, giving direction to the development of a solution. This *character* or theme may be arrived at through the direction of a line, the shape of a space, or the volume. Connecting points in space—such as columns, walls, windows—may be the trigger. Fixed architectural components define the parameters, new elements reshape the spaces. Consideration of program requirements, organization, and aesthetics within the reshaping of space gives form to the character.

The first step is to study the program and examine the site plans. The next several steps involve sketching, sketching, and more sketching. The first thought may be a spontaneous idea for a quick solution—sketch it. It may not be workable or even particularly applicable to the project, but later on it may engender other ideas. Visualize the volumes. Sketch them. Study the plans. Connect architectural features. Create shapes. Give direction. Reread the program. Study the stack of sketches from the beginning. *Become familiar with the building.* There may be cues in the existing shapes, volumes, elements that prod the mind into a new direction. Take note of why a certain feature of a sketch happened: what prompted that shape, direction, volume, material to occur? Gradually, through rereading the program, reviewing the sketches, new, more completely formed ideas and sketches occur and a full-fledged concept takes shape.

Prepare a written concept statement. Whether it is to be presented to the client in written form or orally, writing it down in an organized manner clarifies the thought processes.

**Writing a
Concept
Statement**

The written concept statement might refer to
- ▸ the given architecture of the space and its relationship to the character of the concept
- ▸ specific aspects of the program shown by the client to be of particular importance, such as barrier-free or acoustically treated spaces
- ▸ arrangement of space relative to behavioral or functional aspects
- ▸ character development through color, materials, lighting, and so forth

The concept statement may be developed from notes taken during the sketch process. It should be written in the *future* tense, giving reasons why decisions were made in the development of the visual concept, and stated in terms broad enough to allow client input and refinement through the design development stage.

In the design development stage, the final recommendations for the complete project are developed, and presentations are made to the client for review and approval.
Presentations may include a variety of media and methods.

**Design
Development**

Activities in the design development stage may be
briefly summarized as follows:
- develop and refine the approved conceptual design
- research and consult with jurisdictional authorities regarding
  building and life safety codes, applicable health and liquor
  regulations, and so on
- communicate with necessary specialty consultants
- develop the art, accessories, and graphic/signage programs
- develop and present for client review and approval the final
  design recommendations for space planning, furnishings,
  fixtures, millwork, and all interior surfaces, including lighting,
  electrical, and communication requirements
- refine the budget estimate
- prepare a presentation for client discussion and approval,
  using a variety of media such as drawings, perspectives,
  renderings, color and material boards, photographs, and
  models

When the effort and concentration of obtaining a contract has passed, when the energetic period of programming
is over, and when the creative process of design has been
completed and approved, then the realization of the project
itself gets underway.

**Contract
Documentation**

Accurately communicating the professional solution to
those who will carry out the work is the next vital stage–
specifying what is to be done, obtaining prices from various
sources, and awarding the necessary contracts for completion of the project.

This stage of the designer's work depends on paper.
Over the years, the profession has standardized most of the
vehicles for communication. They can be broadly identified
as *drawings, schedules,* and *specifications.* These are discussed in more detail in the following chapters, but they are
summarized in the chart on page 94.

Drawings, schedules, and written specifications are
instructions on how to physically create the built environment–describing components, quantities, and directions so

that the participants are given enough information to produce the desired results.

When the drawings, schedules, and specifications are complete, they are published–made public–in order to solicit bids from those whose businesses entail the construction and furnishing of the built interior.

The *Call for Tender* for work involving the supply of components or services is detailed in chapters 10 to 12. The tender outlines requirements, the parameters of the work, the time frame for completion of the project, and detailed information regarding terms and conditions.

The Tendering Process

In the tendering process, the designer
▸ prepares for client approval the working drawings and related schedules for interior construction, materials, finishes, furnishings, fixtures, and equipment
▸ coordinates the professional services of specialty consultants and licensed practitioners in the technical areas of mechanical, electrical, and load-bearing design and construction as required for regulatory approvals
▸ identifies the qualified bidders
▸ prepares the bid documents, construction and furnishing specifications
▸ issues addenda as necessary
▸ collects and reviews the bids
▸ assists the client in awarding contracts

Details of the above documents are located further in this book.

Transmittal Forms

Written transmittal forms should accompany all material leaving the design office. They record actions taken by the designer and indicate the action to be taken by others relating to the specific items being transmitted.

The transmittal form should include the following:
▸ design firm name, address, logo, telephone and fax numbers
▸ title of the form: *Transmittal Form* (or similar name)
▸ project name and address
▸ file number
▸ date
▸ name and address of person to receive communication
▸ name of person sending communication
▸ list of items transmitted, such as copy of letter, change order, sepias
▸ quantity of each item
▸ description of each item
▸ indication as to whether the items are attached to the transmittal or sent under separate cover
▸ reason for transmittal
▸ remarks
▸ list of persons to receive copies of items transmitted
▸ signature

Contract Administration

During contract administration, the interior designer
▸ administers the contract documents as the client's agent
▸ confirms that the required permits have been obtained
▸ monitors the contractors'/suppliers' progress as necessary
▸ issues proposed change notices, change orders
▸ conducts periodic site visits and inspections

- reviews and approves shop drawings and samples
- oversees the installation of furnishings, fixtures, and equipment
- reviews the invoices and issues certificates for payment
- prepares a list of deficiencies
- makes final inspection
- prepares the equipment and maintenance manual
- monitors the project through the guarantee period
- completes the termination of contracts

Inevitably, during the course of the contract there will be changes to the project. These must be handled in a formal manner, with supporting written instructions in order to avoid assumptions, confusion, or financial entanglements.

The designer must maintain control of the work through personal supervision and inspection. As work progresses and components are received and installed, the designer should inspect and supervise the project to ensure that requirements have been met. Again, formal communication which keeps the client informed is required.

Having maintained contact with the client and all other concerned parties throughout the project, the designer formalizes project completion with the preparation of a manual for the client. This collection of documents includes guarantees, warranties, maintenance procedures, pertinent names and addresses, and so on.

The designer then monitors the project throughout the warranty/guarantee period (usually one year) to ensure that deficiencies are noted and corrected. Finally, the contracts are reviewed to ensure that they are terminated satisfactorily.

Refer to the following pages for further details:
- Purchase Order–page 120
- Proposed Change Notice–page 120
- Change Order–page 121
- Site Inspection Report–page 121
- Site Supervision Order–page 122
- Certificate for Payment–page 122
- Final Inspection Report–page 123

Warranties and Guarantees

The terms *warranty* and *guarantee* are commonly, but incorrectly, used interchangeably. A *guarantee* is a collateral agreement for the performance of another's undertaking. This most often takes the form of a financial guarantee. The correct term relating to the performance of product is warranty. This is a written statement by the seller that certain facts are as presented. The seller may promise that the product is of a certain quality or will perform in a certain manner. The *warranty* is part of the contract of sale.

All warranties are, or should be, limited with respect to certain conditions such as time, condition of use, and liability. *Fitness for use* is implied in most warranties; that is, the product is sold for a broad category of normal end uses.

Consumer protection laws, locally legislated, may in fact be more stringent than any warranty or lack of warranty provided by a seller of goods. Unless this is specifically excluded in the contract of sale, in most jurisdictions products have implied warranties of being free of manufacturing defects for a reasonable period of time.

Manufacturers' guarantee programs often offer restitution to the purchaser if the item fails to meet stated performance criteria. Labeling, hang tags, or selvage legends on textiles refer to specific warranties, and sometimes to guaranteed finishes.

The client should be made aware of any such programs. Note that anything done to products (such as topical sprays applied to textiles) *after* installation may void the manufacturers' warranties since such actions are outside of their control and can be improperly applied.

Evaluation

Upon completion, all the project's costs should be analyzed and recorded. These figures become models for establishing the costs of proposed projects and the basis for future fees and contracts.

To judge the design's success, a post-occupancy evaluation of the users' satisfaction with the completed project is necessary. This should be undertaken within one to two months of completion. The users' efficiency is affected by their level of satisfaction with the space, and minor irritations may be alleviated through slight adjustments to facilities or planning within this time period. Adaptation takes place after a three- to six-month period. Dissatisfactions become hidden (users "get used to them"), and flawless functioning of the space becomes difficult to achieve.

In the evaluation stage, the designer
▸ reviews and evaluates the design solution after project completion
▸ if retained by owner to do so, conducts a post-occupancy evaluation survey

**Project Analysis
Reports**

The results of evaluation may be recorded on a project analysis report, which should include:
▸ design-firm logo, name, address, telephone and fax numbers
▸ title of the form: *Project Analysis Report*
▸ project name and address
▸ file number
▸ date of report
▸ time frame of project
▸ size of project in square feet (or square meters)
▸ total cost of renovation or new construction
▸ square-foot (or square-meter) cost of construction work
▸ reference to appropriate project information, such as type of planning, open office or conventional
▸ furnishings unit cost
▸ furnishings cost per square foot (or square meter)
▸ square-yard (or square-meter) carpet costs
▸ lineal costs of such components as partitions
▸ cost of design services, expressed as a percentage of total cost and/or expressed as a square-foot (or square-meter) cost
▸ type of fee arrangement,such as percentage fee, fixed fee, or other

JV Associates
1407 Rockford Street
Chicago, Illinois
61954
(312) 987-6543

Time Sheet

Name   Week Ending

Chargeable Time

Project Name	File No.	Code No.	Mon	Tues	Wed	Thurs	Fri	Sat/Sun	Total

Total Chargeable Hours

Non-Chargeable Time

	Mon	Tues	Wed	Thurs	Fri	Sat/Sun	Total
Illness							
Statutory Holidays							
Promotion							
Research							
Personal							
Business Development							
Professional Associations							
Annual Holidays							
Professional Development							
General Office Administration							

Total Non-Chargeable Hours

Total Hours

Breakdown

	Mon	Tues	Wed	Thurs	Fri	Sat/Sun	Total
Normal							
Overtime							

Project Codes

1	Programming	4	Contract Documents	5.3	Site Inspection
2	Conceptual Design	4.1	Working Drawings	6	Evaluation
3	Design Development	4.2	Specifications	7	Project Administration
3.1	Design	4.3	Tender Process	7.1	Client Meeting
3.2	Presentation Drawings	5	Contract Administration	7.2	Consultant Meeting
3.3	Rendering	5.1	Administration	7.3	Contractor Meeting
		5.2	Shop Drawings	8	Travel

Figure 1

JV Associates
1407 Rockford Street
Chicago, Illinois
61954
(312) 987-6543

Prospect Contact Report

Prospect   Date Contacted

Contact   ☐ Telephone Call

Title   ☐ Letter

Phone No.   ☐ Personal Visit

Source of   Date Received
First Information

Type of Business

Nature of Project

Approximate Size

Estimated Cost

Desired Starting Date

Desired Completion Date

Interview Date

Interview Location

Other Designers
Being Considered

Selection Date

Comments

Figure 2

JV Associates
1407 Rockford Street
Chicago, Illlnois
61954
(312) 987-6543

Communication Report

Project   File No.   Date

Page ____ of ____

To   From

Participants

Re:

The above outlines major points discussed. If there are any discrepancies, please notify the writer immediately, otherwise the contents of this report will be viewed as acceptable to all.

Copies to

Signed

Figure 3

JV Associates
1407 Rockford Street
Chicago, Illinois
61954
(312) 987-6543

Transmittal Form

Project   File No.   Date

To   From

Items Transmitted	☐ Attached		☐ Under Separate Cover

	Quantity	Description
☐ Working Drawings		
☐ Sepias		
☐ Prints		
☐ Specifications		
☐ Addendum		
☐ Proposed Change Notice		
☐ Change Order		
☐ Samples		
☐ Shop Drawings		
☐ Copy of Letter		

Reason Transmitted   Remarks

☐ As Requested
☐ For Information
☐ Review and Comment
☐ Approval
☐ Approval as Submitted
☐ Approved as Noted
☐ Correct and Resubmit
☐ Not Approved
☐ Return Signed Original
☐ Copies to
☐ Signed

Copies to

Signed

Figure 4

Inventory Data

JV Associates
1407 Rockford Street
Chicago, Illinois
61954
(312) 987-5543

Project

Department

File No.

Name of Recorder

Date

Page _____ of _____

Room / Person	Item / Description	Color	Size			Condition			Comments	Inventory No.	Relocation
			L	W	H	Good	Fair	Poor			

Figure 5

JV Associates
1407 Rockford Street
Chicago, Illinois
61954
(312) 987-6543

Furnishings Specifications

Project _____   File No. _____   Date _____

Set No. _____   Page ____ of ____

Specification No.	Quantity	Description

Figure 6

JV Associates
1407 Rockford Street
Chicago, Illinois
61954
(312) 987-6543

Furnishings Tender Form

Project _____ **File No.** _____

Page ____ of ____

Specification No.	Quantity	Description	Unit Cost	Extended Cost

Bidder _____ Date _____

Authorizing Signature

Figure 7

JV Associates
1407 Rockford Street
Chicago, Illinois
61954
(312) 987-6543

Addendum

Project	File No.	Date

Addendum No.

To   From

This Addendum is issued prior to the Tender Due Date to revise the Tender/Contract Documents, and as such is part of those documents; the value of all items shall be included in the Tender. After Acceptance of a Tender, claims for cost will not be considered by reason of failure by the Bidder to have read the addenda.

Copies to

Signed

Figure 8

Tendering Document Distribution Record

JV Associates
1407 Rockford Street
Chicago, Illinois
61954
(312) 987-6543

Project _____

File No. _____

Date _____

Set No.	Date Sent	Date Addenda Sent 1 2 3	Bidders Name	Address	Contact Person	Phone No.	Date Bid Deposit Received	Date Bid Deposit Returned

Figure 9

Bid Record

JV Associates
1407 Rockford Street
Chicago, Illinois
61954
(312) 987-6543

Project

File No.

Date

Bidder

Bid Bond Sec. No. Base Bid Price Alternative Manufacturer Price

Item

Figure 10

JV Associates
1407 Rockford Street
Chicago, Illinois
61954
(312) 987-6543

Proposed Change Notice

Project   File No.

Proposed Change Notice No.

To   From

Pursuant to the Conditions of the Contract, the following items are **proposed changes to work** for the above project. **Submit in duplicate** cost of changes, including all sub-contract quotations, as additions or deductions to the Contract price. All labor, material, equipment, and services required to complete the work described shall be provided in accordance with the Contract Documents. Show cost of each item.

Do not proceed with work affected by this P.C.N. until authorized.

Copies to

Signed

Figure 11

JV Associates
1407 Rockford Street
Chicago, Illinois
61954
(312) 987-6543

Change Order

Project   File No.   Date

Change Order No.

To   From

Your proposal for changes (detailed below) has been accepted. This is a written order for you to proceed for the value shown. The contract price will be adjusted accordingly.

Item   Credit   Extra

Subtotal

Revised Contract Amount

Copies to

Signed

Figure 12

JV Associates
1407 Rockford Street
Chicago, Illinois
61954
(312) 987-6543

Site Inspection Report

Project   File No.

Site Inspection   Date of   Date of
Report No.   Inspection   Report

To   From

Items Inspected   Remarks

Copies to

Signed

Figure 13

JV Associates
1407 Rockford Street
Chicago, Illinois
61954
(312) 987-6543

Site Supervision Order

Project	File No.	Date

Site Supervision Order No.

To   From

The following supplemental instructions shall be used to carry out the work. This work shall be done in accordance with the Contract Documents without change in the Contract Time or Contract Sum. If, in the opinion of the Contractor, such instructions or clarifications require work and monies additional to the Contract, notice of same must be provided to the Designer, in writing, prior to work being performed, and in any instance, no later than three working days from receipt of this order.

Copies to

Signed

Figure 14

JV Associates
1407 Rockford Street
Chicago, Illinois
61954
(312) 987-6543

Certificate for Payment

Project   **File No.**   **Date**

Certificate No.

Owner   Contractor

In accordance with the terms of the contract for the above project and the attached application for payment, the named contractor is entitled to payment of the amount stipulated below.

Statement of Contract   **Statement of Payments**

Original contract _____   Work claimed for _____

Extras C.O. no. _____

Credits C.O. no. _____   Hold back % _____

Contract to date _____   Amount payable _____

Value of work _____   Previous certificate(s) _____
done to date

Balance to complete _____   This certificate _____

                                             Total of approved _____
                                             certificates

The Contractor's claim is hereby approved for work done and materials on site, and this Certificate for Payment is approved. This certificate is not negotiable; it is payable only to the payee named herein, and its issuance, payment, and acceptance are without prejudice to any rights of the Owner or Contractor under this Contract.

Design Firm Name   Signed

Figure 15

JV Associates
1407 Rockford Street
Chicago, Illinois
61954
(312) 987-6543

Final Inspection Report

Project   File No.   Date

Report No.

Page _____ of _____

To

Participants

Those items marked deficient must be completed before the Final Certificate for Payment will be issued.

Items Inspected   Complete   Deficiencies

Copies to

Signed

Figure 16

Door Schedule

JV Associates
1407 Rockford Street
Chicago, Illinois
61954
(312) 987-6543

Project

File No.

Date

Page _____ of _____

Door No.	Location	Nominal Size	Type	Material	Core	Finish	UL Label	Type	Material	Finish	Hardware	Remarks

Frame

Figure 17

Room Finish Schedule

JV Associates
1407 Rockford Street
Chicago, Illinois
61954
(312) 987-6543

Project _____

File No. _____

Date _____

Page _____ of _____

Room No.	Name	Floor Material	Floor Finish	Base Material	Base Finish	Height	N/S/E/W	Walls Material	Walls Finish	Ceiling Material	Finish	Height	Remarks

Figure 18

Shop Drawing Record

JV Associates
1407 Rockford Street
Chicago, Illinois
61954
(312) 987-6543

Project

File No.

Submitted By	Description	Person Checking	Date Received	Date Returned	Revise & Resubmit	Approv'd As Noted	Approv'd

Figure 19

JV Associates
1407 Rockford Street
Chicago, Illinois
61954
(312) 987-6543

Statement

Project			File No.		Date		

To			From				

Date	Person Involved	Description of Work			Hours	Rate	Total

Summary

Invoiced Previously _____

Credits _____

Balance Owing _____

This Invoice _____

Amount Owed _____

Signed

Figure 20

Programming

9

The *program* is a general term for the information that is accumulated prior to embarking on a particular design project. To assemble this aggregation of detail into a usable body of knowledge is to *write the program.*

If a facility is to satisfy both the client's expectations and the users' needs, the designer must identify these desires clearly, must know the client and understand the users.

On occasion, the client will supply a prepared program; the following may then act as a checklist by which to assess the client's information. The client may not have probed with sufficient depth into such details as the functional needs of each space or individual, and the socio-cultural or behavioral needs of the users.

Since the program is the primary source of input into the design stage, the quality of the program has a direct influence on the quality of the design.

The programming system described in this chapter, with additional forms, charts, graphs, sketches, and so on, is too involved in its entirety for use on small projects but, in principle, acts as a guideline to the pre-design stage.

Preliminary Activity

Before signing a contract with the client, discuss writing the program. This process, which may need to be explained to the client, can take up to one-third of the total hours allocated to the project, however, a thorough program prevents wasted time and errors in design. Designer and client must agree on how this activity is to be performed.

Confirm that the client's designated contact has the authority to assist the designer's research and to make decisions based on it.

Identify the project objectives: are they to improve a current situation, to anticipate future needs, or to develop an image for the future?

Compare alternative courses of action with a view to feasibility and resource availability. Do the plans call for remodeling of existing space, leasing new space, or constructing a new facility? Comparison of alternative sites may clarify objectives and establish sound reasons why one is better than the others.

Prepare a plan of the existing premises, locating all furniture, fixtures, equipment, and personnel. This is necessary to answer the questions, "What exists now?" and "What is wrong with the present facility?"

Gathering Information

Gathering information is the first activity associated with programming. All areas must be studied:
- the client
- the users of the space
- the space itself
- the site

Programming Checklist

The following checklist would be applicable to a fairly large project for a business client; it is sufficiently generic to adapt to most design contracts.

Heeding the "design is for people" dictum, the majority of programming activity is focused on the users of the space.

The Client
- What does the client do or provide?
- What specific goods or services are supplied by the company?
- What activities will take place on the premises?
- What is the hierarchical structure of the company? (The designer may ask for an organizational structure chart.)
- What is the decision-making route?
- How do individuals and departments relate to each other?
- What is the company's five-year plan? ten-year plan?
- Is the company likely to outgrow these new facilities, or will extra space be built in to allow for future growth?
- Is there a new direction in technology that could have an impact on future growth, hardware changes or new requirements, organizational structures, and so on?

The Users
- Who will be using the facilities? Employees? Visitors? Group employees into departments; identify the number of employees, job titles, and categories.
- Do expansion factors need to be built in?
- Identify the number and frequency of visitors.

Activities
- What does each employee do? Identify through job descriptions the activities which must be considered, their time and duration.
- Similarly, identify the activities of visitors.

In designing corporate facilities, recording this information may involve several forms or charts of considerable complexity. This information is likely to be the key to efficient functioning of the facility.

Behavioral Needs

▸ What are the privacy needs inherent in each job description or required by each individual?

▸ How clearly should territories be defined for the group and the individual?

▸ Are places required where people can be brought together in formal or informal settings?

▸ Is there an appropriate form, or spatial shape and volume that, through cultural cues, will allow employees and visitors alike to feel comfortable?

Space Requirements

▸ What spaces are required to support the activities and needs of the users?

▸ Identify every type of space or room needed. This initial list should be as complete as possible but will be refined as the programming progresses. Subsequent evaluations may lead to the elimination of some spaces and the addition of others. Include an estimated gross area for each space, and any requirements for a particular shape, volume, or dimension.

Furnishings and Equipment

▸ What furnishings and equipment–built in, fixed in place, set in place, or mobile–are needed for each space or room identified?

▸ What are the current conditions? Are the existing furnishings, fixtures, and equipment types satisfactory, or is something additional needed?

▸ Refer to the checklist for recording existing conditions (page 103).

Environmental Factors

▸ Are there any special requirements for HVAC (heating, ventilation, and air conditioning)?

▸ What particular acoustic conditions are likely to occur?

▸ What will be needed to create the appropriate acoustic ambience?

▸ Identify the illumination requirements–ambient, task, and feature

▸ Are there any special electrical loads due to equipment in particular areas?

Safety

▸ Will any activity, user group, or piece of equipment require special safety conditions?

▸ Are special surface treatments necessary?

▸ What are durability and materials-maintenance factors in the spaces?

▸ Consider graphic identification of areas and signage.

Circulation Patterns

▸ Who exchanges information and how is it done? Chart the movement of information by telephones, fax, mail, and conversation both for individuals and groups.

▸ Circulation of users is important to the zoning of departments and to the sizes of pathways. A matrix showing the relationship between departments should be developed.

▸ Does movement of equipment affect circulation patterns?

Developing the Program

Develop configurations for spaces using the *bubble diagram* technique, based on the information gathered on user activities, circulation, gross areas, and so on.

Initial Space Planning

List all furnishings, equipment, storage, and users to be located in each space, including adjacency needs.

From the bubble diagram and the list, simple preliminary space and furnishings layouts may be developed. Behavioral needs such as *orientation* and *sense of place* should be kept in mind.

Analysis of Program

Organize all the research data into clearly understood charts, graphs, graphics, lists, and so on.

Reorder all the data, category by category, for each space or room in the program. Analyze each space and assign priority relative to functional planning.

Program Presentation

Present the program to the client for approval, explaining that it is not static and is subject to change as further needs arise. However, at this stage the program and its analysis are the basis for development of the initial budget.

Preliminary Budget

Develop a preliminary budget, based on the client's wishes and the program. It may be necessary to develop a budget for *new* furnishings and equipment to compare with a budget which reuses everything existing that is in good-to-excellent condition. In the latter case, costs for refurbishing must be included.

Budget Presentation

Present the clearly stated budget or budget options to the client, explaining precisely what is included.

Existing Conditions Record

A project which involves the reuse of a building requires a descriptive record of the existing conditions. This record provides a basis for estimating the extent of project work and costs. A portion of the form might include a grid where a plan and/or elevations of the existing space may be sketched easily and quickly.

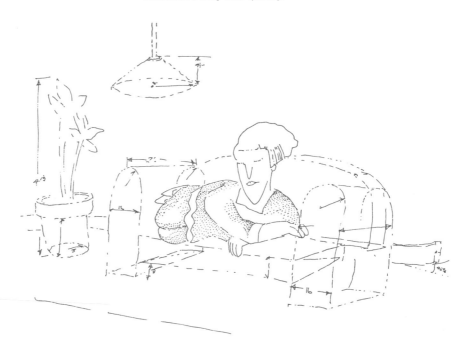

The existing conditions record should include the following:

▸ design firm logo, name, address, telephone and fax numbers
▸ title of the form: *Existing Conditions Record*
▸ project name and address
▸ file number
▸ date
▸ name of person recording the conditions
▸ page number of total number of pages
▸ room number and name, and name of department
▸ floor: material and color
▸ base: material, color, and height
▸ walls: (north, east, south, west) material and color
▸ ceiling: material, color, and height
▸ cabinetry: lower cupboards, upper cupboards, top cupboards–material, color, and height
▸ doors and windows: type, material, color, and dimensions
▸ frames/trim: material and color (of each), hardware
▸ utilities: heating, ventilation, air conditioning, plumbing, electrical
▸ lighting: type, direction of light, type of fixtures, designer's evaluation of quality of existing lighting fixtures
▸ comments
▸ sketch (indicate scale)

It may be necessary or desirable to photograph the existing spaces. The photographs should then be keyed by number to the form.

A project involving the reuse of existing furnishings and equipment requires a complete inventory of all items. Continuity in the method of recording this information is important. The form should include a column where new locations of existing furnishings can be recorded, or discards noted.

Many design firms complete an inventory of existing furnishings even for those projects where all the furnishings will be new. The inventory is helpful in assessing the existing *use* of furnishings and equipment.

Inventory Data Form

The inventory data form should include the following:

▸ design firm logo, name, address, telephone and fax numbers
▸ title of the form: *Inventory Data Form*
▸ project name and address
▸ file number
▸ date
▸ page number of total number of pages
▸ name of person recording the inventory
▸ room number and/or person who is currently using the items
▸ item description
▸ color
▸ dimensions
▸ condition of existing item (for example, *good, fair, poor*)
▸ comments
▸ inventory number
▸ new location

It may be necessary or desirable to photograph existing items. In that case, include a column listing a cross-reference to the photograph number.

Furnishings
Specifications

10

A specifications document is one of many legal instruments used in interior design. It adds to the body of information contained in the contract and in the various working drawings, schedules, shop drawings, and other technical criteria particular to the built-environment industry. People who *write* specifications are communicating facts and instructions. People who *read* specifications must be able to understand these directives easily, with no need to interpret or guess at meanings. It is a mark of professionalism to learn and practice excellence in specifications writing.

Furnishings specifications are written contract documents which may include, as applicable, detailed information on
- furniture
- accessories
- window treatments
- movable luminaires
- carpets
- artwork
- plants and planters

Purpose and Use of Specifications

Specifications are used for two different but related purposes: to indicate what is needed in order to elicit quotations of price and time, and to guide the successful bidders in the implementation of the design solution.

Specifications, as **invitations to tender**
- identify the parties involved in the project and their respective responsibilities
- instruct bidders on procedure
- outline general conditions of the contract
- outline procedure and method of payment
- clarify quantity and quality of items required
- describe the items, work, material required

Specifications, as **guidelines for implementation**,
- ensure that the above requirements are met
- ensure that the items meet product standards
- legalize contractual arrangements

Types of Bidding Systems

Specifications may be broadly classified as *closed* or *open*.

A *closed* specification calls for an exact item by stock or style number and by brand name, thus discouraging the consideration of any other product.

An *open* specification allows choice between several products through the use of an open *alternative clause*, by specifying certain approved alternatives.

Closed– Manufacturer's Bid (or Base Bid)

This type of closed specification identifies particular products. The designer includes the manufacturer's name and the stock number, and lists all the information necessary to price the product, place purchase orders, and ensure that the manufacturers meet their own published quality standards.

It may include all or part of the manufacturer's specification, or refer to same in the designer's specifications.

Designers use this type of specification in order to
► have full control over the products used in the project
► facilitate the preparation of detailed design work based on the selected products
► save time and effort by using the manufacturer's data
► simplify the bidding procedures by eliminating multiple assessment and selection

Open–Bidder's Choice

This type of open specification allows a choice between designated products that have been determined as equivalent to each other, or that have been considered as acceptable alternatives.

One method of handling this type of specification is to list one product by brand name, stock number, and description, and then establish the requirements and standards for the specified item. Alternatives may then be proposed by the bidders and "weighed" against the criteria implicitly established by the item specified.

Bidder's choice is a more time-consuming specifications process, both in writing additional criteria and in selecting and evaluating alternatives. Designers should also be aware that controversy sometimes develops when opinions about products' equivalency differ.

Open–Descriptive Specification

This type of open specification does not use manufacturers' names or stock numbers. The designer describes the product required in considerable detail. This may include how the product is to be constructed, all material information and performance standards, as well as general descriptions of dimensions, components, color, finish, and so forth.

Performance standards are recommended for inclusion when the desired performance level can be evaluated by valid standards and testing methods for such specifications as carpet or drapery.

On occasion the client and the supplier(s) agree on an equitable system of supplying the specified goods, and negotiate prices on all items and installation involved in the project. These negotiations are conducted in confidence and exact terms are not made common knowledge.

These are directions to the bidder about what to bid on, how to submit the tender, and specific terms related to the project.

Specifications

Tenders   Identify to whom the tender documents must be delivered (usually the designer), and the date and time by which they must be received. It is important to adhere to a specific time so that there cannot be any claim that one bidder was favored over another by having a longer period of time to complete the tender.

Instructions to Bidders

Supply the bidders with copies of the tender form, which lists the items to be bid upon, and state how many copies must be contained in the submission. The bidders' submissions should be sealed in opaque envelopes to prevent prior-knowledge claims, and identified on the outside by the bidder's name, project name and file number, and sections or items included in the tender.

Identify whether bidders must tender on all sections, one or more complete sections, or separate items. (Refer to *Sectioning of Specifications*, page 115.)

Include a requirement that the final total be in words as well as figures, so that there is no opportunity for error. Tenders with erasures, white-outs, qualifiers, or other alterations should not be accepted. The tender must be signed by an authorized officer of the bidding company.

To allow the client flexibility in making a decision, it should be stated that "lowest or any tender not necessarily accepted."

Unit Prices   The owner may wish to increase or decrease the number of units of a given item. This could cause changes to the pricing and should be clarified for the bidder.

Example of possible wording:

"All adjustments in the quantities of items specified shall be based on *unit prices* quoted in the Tender. The Owner does not undertake to purchase any or all of the items specified. Where the unit price varies due to quantity, legitimate price adjustments may be made by the Contractor. Within ninety (90) days after award of contract, additional requirements in excess of those specified may be purchased by the Owner at a unit price based on landed net cost, plus 10 percent, plus installation costs."

Non-Compliance   Non-compliance with any condition or instruction noted is cause for rejection of a tender.

Taxes   It is imperative to include a clause in reference to the inclusion or exclusion of federal or local taxes. Check with the nearest taxation department for current information. Some corporate and institutional clients may have special tax concessions.

Validity of Tender   State the length of time that the bid price is to be held valid. This is customarily thirty days but may vary on occasion.

Access to Premises   If the premises are in a building under construction or already built, access for the purpose of measuring must be given to the bidders through arrangement with the general contractor or the building management. Directives for gaining access should be included.

Bid Deposit   Plans and specifications are expensive and may be reused after the bidding process. To ensure the return of these by the unsuccessful bidders a *bid deposit* of "x" dollars should be required.

Example of possible wording:

"Bidders shall deposit $_____ per set of plans and specifications with the Designer in the form of a certified cheque. This deposit shall be returned when the plans and specifications are returned in good condition within fifteen (15) days after the closing date of tenders."

Examination of Documents and Premises   The responsibility of reading the documents carefully and examining the site must be borne by the bidder. To prevent misunderstandings, this should be stated clearly.

Example of possible wording:

"a) Bidders shall familiarize themselves with all drawings, specifications, documents, and site conditions, and shall satisfy themselves of all pertinent conditions prior to tendering. No extra charges shall be allowed for failure to do this. Drawings and specifications shall be treated as complementary, and what is called for by one is as binding as if called for by all.

b) Any discrepancies, errors, or omissions shall be brought to the attention of the Designer before submission of Tender, otherwise the Designer shall be the sole judge of their interpretation.

c) All communications between Owner, Designer, and Bidder shall be in writing. No oral instructions shall be binding on any of these parties. Written addenda or corrections issued during the time of bidding shall be considered as part of the specifications and shall become part of the contract instructions."

Product Approval Standard   In a closed bid-contract, it is necessary to state that tenders are to be based on the specified materials and no equivalents will be accepted unless already included in the specifications.

In an open-bid contract, equivalent items may already be included on the tender form, or they may be accepted on application by a qualified bidder during the tendering time.

Alternatives   An alternative product or material is one which is not viewed as exactly equal to the unit specified, but is acceptable for consideration as a substitute. This situation requires very careful handling since it opens up possibilities for outside pressures to be applied to the bidder and the owner.

Example of possible wording:

"a) Requests for alternatives may be submitted for approval no later than five working days before Tenders are due. These requests shall be made in duplicate, in writing, and the Applicant shall be prepared to produce full specifications, samples, and so on, as may be required by the Designer.

b) Approval, if given, will be no less than three working days before Tenders are due.

c) No application for alternatives will be entertained unless submitted by an authorized Bidder.

d) There shall be no alternatives considered to the colors and finishes as specified herein."

Standard of Excellence   Protection is needed against incomplete or improper work or installation, or products which do not follow the manufacturer's specifications.

Example of possible wording:

"a) The Bidder shall be responsible for a complete job in any section or as otherwise noted. This shall mean supply and installation of all elements specified in the positions shown on the layout drawings and fully ready for use. On manufactured items, all work, construction, or installation shall be in accordance with the Manufacturer's directions.

b) Deviation from standard shall be considered sufficient reason for rejection by the Designer. The Designer shall furnish written reason for rejection, but the opinion of the Designer shall be final."

Samples   It is sometimes necessary to require samples of furniture or materials for examination by the designer and/or owner. If alternatives are involved it is highly recommended. At the same time, it is also important not to allow this to be unreasonable for the bidder. If the designer or the owner intends to damage the items or submit them to any unusual conditions or circumstances during examination, this should be brought to the attention of the bidder in writing.

Example of possible wording:

"a) All Bidders shall be required to have samples of all tendered items available two weeks after close of Tender, if requested by the Owner.

b) When requested, the sample(s) shall be delivered to a location designated by the Designer. Unless otherwise designated by the Designer, the Bidder shall assume responsibility for the sample(s) from point of shipment to return. On receipt of notice from the Designer, Bidders shall remove the sample(s) within two weeks, at their own expense."

Delivery Date   A date should be stipulated for delivery of the furnishings. The installation date may be at the time of delivery or later, depending on the project circumstances.

Bid Bond   To ensure that a bidder holds to his or her tendered price, a bond—usually amounting to 10 percent of the tender—is requested. This is held in escrow until the contracts have been awarded.

General Conditions of Contract

This portion of the contract document gives all pertinent information and direction regarding the legal aspects of the contract between the client and the successful contractor(s). It becomes part of the contract when signed by both parties.

An initial clause identifies all parties concerned: owner, general contractor, design firm, (all with addresses), and the name, location, and file number of the project.

Guarantees   Depending on the scope of the project, it may be necessary to require a *performance bond* of the successful contractor. On large projects it can be very costly to the owner if the contractor delays the work unduly, or simply does not perform—in which case the project may have to be turned over to another contractor, usually at a higher price.

Example of possible wording:

"a) The Contractor shall furnish a *Performance Bond* amounting to 50 percent of the contract sum, and maintain it in force for one full year after the final Certificate of Payment.

b) Final payments shall not absolve the Contractor from liability for defective workmanship, or other faults, for a full year after completion, or for the effects of same that may appear after this period due to fraudulent conduct by the Contractor or his or her Sub-contractor.

c) If the Manufacturer's standard guarantee is longer, then it shall apply in addition to the above.

d) Any defect in material or workmanship shall be promptly rectified by the Contractor without cost to the Owner during this period."

Liability Insurance   Accident insurance can be an important issue, particularly on large projects. It may be advisable even on relatively small ones.

Example of possible wording:

"A Contractor's Liability Certificate shall be filed with the Designer before the work is started. Include liability insurance up to [$1,000,000 or more]. File required Certificates with the Designer before the work is commenced, including a statement that cancellation will not be effected without ten days prior notice being given to the Owner."

Fire Insurance   It should be noted that fire insurance is the responsibility of the contractor *before* the owner has received the goods, and the responsibility of the owner *after* receipt of the goods. If the owner has the furnishings stored on the premises, arrangements should be made with the building contractor in the case of new construction, or the building owner or agent in the case of an existing building.

Lien   Suppliers and sub-contractors may issue a lien against the owner's premises or property if they have not been paid by the contractor. To protect the owner from liens, on receipt of payment the contractor should issue a declaration that all suppliers and sub-contractors have been paid to date. Various government jurisdictional levels have differing regulations regarding liens. It is necessary to check these regulations carefully for each project.

Shop Drawings   For custom work, the designer usually requests shop drawings to be submitted by the manufacturer or sub-contractor. The designer must be aware that approval of shop drawings means acceptance of liability, along with the supplier of the drawings, for errors or omissions.
Example of possible wording:

"a) The Contractor shall submit shop drawings if requested by the Designer. No work shall be undertaken until such shop drawings have been approved in writing.
b) Approval of shop drawings shall not imply release of the Contractor's responsibility for checking dimensions and conditions.
c) After approval, four sets of shop drawings shall be furnished: two sets for checking and two sets for records (with amendments where necessary); or shop drawings shall be submitted as sepia transparency prints (four sets, as above)."

Work Changes   Most projects undergo some changes. It is necessary to identify clearly the process by which changes will be handled.
Example of possible wording:

"a) No changes in work shall take place without written authorization from the Designer. Any detail drawings issued after acceptance of the bid that involve extra work, shall be issued as a Proposed Change Notice. The Contractor shall not proceed with any work until a Change Order has been authorized by the Owner.
b) Amounts of extra costs or credits asked for by the Proposed Change Notice shall be itemized in a form such as the Designer may direct. These shall only become effective as extras to, or deductions from, the contract amount, after receipt by the Contractor of the Designer's signed Change Order.
c) To facilitate checking, applications for payment must itemize all extras and credits. In the applications for payment, cover the Contractor's work in the month during which such extra work is done; cover Sub-contractors' work in the month following its completion."

Payment Application   For purposes of checking requests for payment against a contractor's invoice, it is easier if the invoices are sent to the designer. However, some owners prefer to have them sent to their in-house purchasing agent. This routing should be noted.

Invoicing Invoices should be submitted by the contractor at the end of each month for goods delivered and/or installed in that month.

The contractor may expect payment of
▶ eighty percent of monies payable thirty days after delivery
▶ ten percent thirty days after installation
▶ ten percent within thirty days after final acceptance by the designer

The major portion of the cost is payable after delivery even though it may be some time before items are installed. This gap between delivery and installation is usually caused by delays in the construction and finishing work, and it is unreasonable to hold back all monies from one contractor for delays caused by someone else.

Assignment Contractors may wish to assign the project to a firm other than the one selected for various financial reasons. This should not be allowed without the written permission of the designer. Including a clause to this effect will allow the designer to ensure that there is no infringement of the rights of the owner.

Storage Most contracts call for furnishings to be *drop-shipped*, that is, delivered directly to the site rather than to a storage building. This must be carefully considered due to the unpredictability of site readiness to receive the goods. Costs are usually separated into those chargeable to the contractor, and those to the owner.
Example of possible wording:

"a) The Contractor shall be responsible for scheduling the deliveries and work so that the merchandise can be drop-shipped on the specified date, on the Premises, and received by the Owner or the Owner's agent.

b) An area shall be assigned to hold the furnishings, as they are received, for storage and assembly. The Owner shall be responsible for making this area secure.

c) In the event that goods are shipped early, the Contractor shall bear the cost of any storage and handling costs.

d) In the event that the Premises shall not be made available at the allotted date, handling and storage costs shall be considered as an extra. Such an extra shall only be granted upon verification by the Contractor of incurred handling and storage charges, in the form of receipts, vouchers, and so on.

e) All furnishings shall be carefully protected by the Contractor on the Premises, until accepted by the Owner as complete, installed, and ready to use."

Damage Most transportation companies require damage claims to be made within a very few days of acceptance of a shipment. Damage to cartons can be seen and checked on arrival; concealed damage is more difficult to handle.

On large consignments it is impractical, and often impossible, to open every carton, particularly when the goods have to be moved again for installation. Arrangements for later checking and claims should be made before acceptance of a shipment.

Damage to the surfaces of the premises can happen during installation. The contractor should be cautioned about this and instructed that, prior to installation, all building surfaces where furniture or furnishings are to be transported and placed should be examined, and any existing marks or defects drawn to the attention of the designer in writing. The contractor shall carefully protect existing and finished work from damage during the installation. All work and furniture or furnishings damaged during installation shall be made good at the contractor's expense.

Conditions of Site   The designer should keep in mind that there are likely to be site-access restrictions such as doorway sizes, elevators, and hallways. This should be drawn to the attention of the contractor, and responsibilities identified.

Example of possible wording:

"a) Before installation of articles in this contract, the Contractor shall examine all locations on the Premises where the items are to be located. The Contractor shall advise the Designer in writing of any conditions that would adversely affect the proper and satisfactory installation. The Designer shall give approval in writing before the Contractor proceeds with the work.

b) Additional costs incurred by the Contractor due to unforeseeable difficulties in delivery or installation, such as elevator or hoist services, restricted hours for delivery, or off-loading due to access conditions to Premises, shall be chargeable as an extra to the Contract upon proof of such costs in the form of vouchers, receipts, and so on. The above does not relieve the Contractor from the responsibility of observing *Instructions to Bidders–Examination of Documents and Premises*."

Installation   Interior designers become furniture movers at some time on every project. However, to simplify this activity the contractor should be given explicit instructions in this regard. Coding each item on the drawings and requiring cartons to be similarly coded can assist greatly. On large projects this becomes a necessity. Since packaging materials are usually a fire hazard, cleanliness of the site should be emphasized.

Example of possible wording:

"a) Furniture installation plans will be given to the Contractor. Each item shall be installed, located in accordance with the final furniture plan.

b) The Contractor shall mark all cartons and items for delivery to the correct areas as indicated on the installation plan.

c) The Contractor shall remove from the Premises all cartons and packing and leave floors broom-clean (daily, if required).

d) The Contractor shall keep all entrances and exits clear and clean at all times.

e) Upon receipt of the goods by the Owner, all items shall be free of marks, stains, or dirt, and in first-class condition."

Final Inspection   A preliminary and a final inspection by the designer, contractor, and the owner (at least for the final inspection) shall be made. Further inspections due to faults of the contractor may be unreasonable, and if required, charged to the contractor.

Example of possible wording:

"a) One preliminary and one final inspection on completion of the installation shall be made by the Designer.

b) Should further inspections become necessary due to faulty workmanship or non-adherence to the specifications or the intent of the specifications, the Designer or a representative reserves the right to charge the Contractor for time and expenses. These costs shall be deducted from monies owed to the Contractor by the Owner."

Termination of Contract   Terms under which the contract may be terminated should also be spelled out.

Example of possible wording:

"Should the Contractor become insolvent, fail to supply work or materials specified, or be under any liens for unpaid labor or materials supplied in connection with the project, the Designer is entitled to exercise certain rights:

a) to stop the work on notice to the Contractor, and to bar the Contractor and his or her employees from the Premises

b) to supply the balance of labor and materials to complete the work, with cost of such labor and materials deducted from any monies due to the Contractor under this Contract

c) to appoint and employ a Supervisor of the work whose wages and expenses shall be deductible from any monies due, or to become due, to the Contractor under this Contract; this Supervisor to have absolute authority over the balance of the work required and over the substitute Contractor and/or the employees employed to complete such work"

Maintenance and Instructions   The designer may require the contractor to provide the owner with applicable available information covering the proper use and maintenance of the items supplied under the contract. This may be required before the final payment is released.

Definitions

Within the specifications document, it is customary to list standard definitions. Any particular words or phrases should also be defined here.

Common Specification Terms

Alternative   an item or product of similar utility which the Owner agrees to consider instead of that which was specified

Bidder   one who submits a Tender

Change Order   authorization to proceed with work outlined on Proposed Change Notice (PCN) at price submitted

Contractor   the successful bidder

Designer   the person who, acting as the Owner's Agent, proposes the scheme

Drop-shipment   delivery of merchandise to the Premises

Equivalent   a similar product having characteristics conforming rigidly, in the opinion of the Designer, to the quality standard required by the specifications

General Building Contractor   the Contractor in charge of erecting or renovating the building

Manufacturer   the firm engaged in making the merchandise

Premises   the building, particularly the inside or that part specifically under construction

Owner   the client for whom the project is commissioned

Proposed Change Notice (PCN)   itemized list of proposed changes to the Contract (with request for changes in price, if any)

Sections   units of merchandise grouped together for the purpose of tendering

Site   the land on which the structure is built and land immediately adjoining this, or that portion of a building in which the Premises are to be located

Supplier   the agent from whom the Contractor obtains the merchandise

Tender   a proposal to undertake specific work or to supply goods, at a stated rate or fee

The list of manufacturers and distributors should be included in alphabetical order, and clearly identified in conjunction with the required product. Spellings, addresses, and, if appropriate, names of contact persons, must be accurate.

List of Manufacturers and Distributors

In order to ensure the client the most competitive prices, it is customary to divide all of the items that are required for the project into groups of similar-type products. This allows the manufacturers and/or suppliers to bid only on those groups that are within their normal area of business. For example, office furniture dealers can provide competitive prices on desks, chairs, and files, not on hospital beds. A desk manufacturer may be able to offer lower prices on desks, but the chair that the designer has specified may be produced by a different company.

Sectioning of Specifications

Furnishings specifications are usually divided into the following general sections. The headings suggest suitable groupings; specific sections to suit a particular project may be required.

Section 1 Lounge Furniture
Section 2 Tables
Section 3 Office Desks
Section 4 Office Chairs
Section 5 Files
Section 6 Beds
Section 7 Carpets
Section 8 Drapery
Section 9 Blinds
Section 10 Portable Lamps
Section 11 Miscellaneous

Suppliers of goods and services (the prospective bidders) are provided with detailed lists of requirements on a furnishings specifications form. The following checklists may be used in the preparation of this material.

Specifications Checklist

The following information is required in the preparation of a furnishings specification:

▸ correct item name
▸ catalog number
▸ item number

Furniture

▸ quantity required
▸ description:
    components
    dimensions
    color
    material
    finish
▸ manufacturers' more fully detailed specifications
▸ description of custom designs and reference to appropriate drawings
▸ shipping instructions
▸ installation instructions
▸ list of sources and addresses

Drapery

The following is an outline of the information that is usually required in the preparation of a drapery specification:

▸ area:
    location
    approximate measurements
    elevation description
▸ material:
    name and manufacturer
    pattern number and description
    color number and description
    fiber content
▸ characteristics:
    colorfast
    yarn-dyed
    sunrot-resistant
    shrink-proof
    fade-resistant
    washable
    others, as required
▸ make-up:
    type of pleat
    fullness
    header size and description; type of stiffening
    hem size and dimensions
    type of seams
▸ hardware:
    type of track, weight
    type of hooks
    type of pull system (specify all necessary materials and
       methods to ensure a first-class installation)
▸ installation:
    explicit instructions as to ceiling or wall installation
    type of ceiling or wall material or construction
    to be hung as single panel, pair of panels, center split,
       pull left, or pull both ways?
    special instructions (for example, *finished-looking
       appearance both sides*)
▸ list of sources and addresses

Carpet

The following is an outline of the information that is usually required in the preparation of a carpet specification:

▸ area:
    location
    approximate dimensions

- material:
    - name and brand
    - pattern number and description
    - color number and description
    - fiber content
    - weight of pile (including weights of the top yarn only and the total weight)
    - rows per inch
    - pitch
    - characteristics
- backing:
    - type and weight
    - characteristics
- underpad:
    - type and weight
    - characteristics
- installation
    - description: wall-to-wall or area; room size
    - type: tackless, glued, or fringed
    - floor material or construction
    - instructions as to one-way patterns or piles
    - type of seams
    - reference to location of seams noted on layout drawings
    - instructions for doorways, edges, or unusual situations
    - preparatory work
    - restretching
    - specifications for all necessary fittings to ensure a first-class installation
    - clean-up and maintenance instructions
- list of sources and addresses

The Specifications Document

Specifications are usually published as a separate document. The standard format is outlined below.

Cover   The cover states that the document contains the specifications of work to be done, materials and furnishings to be supplied for the named project, as well as the statement that the specifications and any accompanying drawings have been prepared by, or under the supervision of, the design firm. It will also include a file number, copy number, and the date of publication.

Table of Contents   The table of contents of the specifications book lists the several divisions with page numbers:
- Instructions to Bidders
- General Conditions of Contract
- Definitions
- Manufacturers (names and addresses for items specified)
- Tender Forms
- List of Drawings
- Custom Detail Sheets (if applicable)

Physical Format for Specifications

In developing the physical format of the specifications the following criteria should be considered:
- consistency of layout
- organization of material for easy reference through thoughtful use of headings, spacing, size and design of type, underlining, and location on page
- logical sequence

- clear and consistent page numbering (for clarity, each page should also refer to the section number, the page number of that section, and the total number of pages in the section, for example, 3:9/15–which means Section 3, page 9 of 15 pages)
- good design, incorporating such details as sufficient binding allowance and margins for notes
- sources in alphabetical order and their addresses

Specifications Language

Specifications are prepared as work on the drawings progresses, using standard, plain language, with care taken not to either *overspecify* or *underspecify*. When the text is prepared, the specifications document must be written, then reviewed carefully for content, intent, and typographical errors–and then checked again!

Information should be given *once only* and should be located in the most logical place. Subsequent reference to the information notes its location.

Specifications should not be ambiguous. Language exists to make meaning clear.

The traditional way to write specifications is in the *indicative* mood: "The carpet shall be secured to the floor with adhesive." A more recent alternative is to write such directions in the *imperative*: "Secure carpet to the floor with adhesive." Either form is correct and both are explicit. Whatever the choice, the designer must be consistent within a given set of specifications.

Some words tend to be misused:
- shall/will–*shall* designates a command, *will* implies a choice
- either–*either* means one or the other; it is sometimes mistakenly used to indicate *both*
- amount/quantity–*amount* is imprecise, *quantity* is measurable
- any–*any* implies choice; sometimes it is mistakenly used to indicate *all*
- and/or, etc.–*and/or, etc.* implies choice or uncertainty: do not use in specifications

As in contracts, capitalized words and terms–*the Contractor, the Premises,* and so on–are used to designate the previously identified "particulars."

Tender Form

The tender form is provided by the designer as part of the specifications. It is a list of the specified items on which tendered prices are entered. The tender form includes the following details:
- design firm: logo, name, address, telephone and fax numbers
- title of the form: *Furnishings Tender Form*
- project name and address
- file number
- item number
- catalog number
- name of the item
- quantity required

As well, space is left for the bidder to fill in the
- unit price
- extended price (unit price multiplied by the quantity)

- section total
- sales taxes (if applicable)
- final total for the section
- signature of authorized representative of the firm

The form may also request specific information from the bidder regarding estimated time allowance for production of goods and for installation.

The tender form may be a separate listing at the end of each section, or may be set up in columns located beside the furnishings description.

If a change is required to the specifications prior to the due date of the bids, the designer issues an addendum to all bidders. All addenda become part of the contract documents.

Addendum

The addendum form should include:
- design firm: logo, name address, telephone and fax numbers
- title of the form: *Addendum*
- number of issue: first addendum, second, and so on
- project name and address
- file number
- date
- name of bidder to whom addendum is being issued
- name of person sending the form
- distribution of copies: owner, bidders, appropriate consultants (if involved)
- signature

The Construction Specifications Institute suggests that addendum may be used for the following changes:
- in the date, time, and location for receipt of bids
- in the required quality of work
- in the sequence of installation or method of installation
- to include additional qualified products or additional standards affecting performance
- in scheduled completion dates

This list is never inclusive because there are many other situations when an addendum may be required.

During the bidding phase of a project, a record is kept of all persons who receive the documents for bidding purposes. This record might also note the receipt and return of bid deposits.

**Tendering
Document
Distribution
Record**

This record requires completion of the following information:
- design firm: logo, name, address, telephone and fax numbers
- title of the form: *Tendering Document Distribution Record*
- project name and address
- file number
- number of each set of documents (set number)
- distribution date of each set of documents (date sent)
- distribution date of each addendum (date addendum sent)
- bidders' names, addresses, telephone and fax numbers (the firms to which each set of documents were sent)
- name of contact person with each bidder's firm
- date of receipt of each bid deposit
- date of return of each bid deposit

Bid Records

All bidders must adhere to the bidding system that is set forth in the *Instructions to Bidders* section of the specifications documents (pages 107–110).

Irregularities may have legal ramifications, therefore a careful record should be kept of the receipt of bids: date, bid bond submission, and the amount of the bid. This should accompany a communication report which includes the names of persons present at the time of the opening of the tenders.

The bid record requires completion of the following information:
▸ design firm: logo, name, address, telephone and fax numbers
▸ title of the form: *Bid Record*
▸ project name and address
▸ file number
▸ date when bids were opened
▸ firm names of all bidders
▸ indication of receipt of bid bond from each bidder
▸ number of the specification section
▸ price of items as specified (base bid price)
▸ if items are not as specified, the recorded alternatives (item, manufacturer, price)

Purchase Order

The purchase order is a legal agreement between the owner and the contractor (who is the successful bidder) whereby both parties agree to the terms and conditions as outlined in the specification documents, and agree to the tendered price.

The purchase order is accompanied by a copy of the general conditions as set forth in the legal portion of the specifications and the pertinent section(s) of the itemized specifications.

A purchase order should include:
▸ design firm: logo, name, address, telephone and fax numbers
▸ title of the form: *Purchase Order*
▸ project name and address
▸ file number
▸ date
▸ owner's name and address
▸ name and address of the successful supplier or contractor to whom the purchase order is being sent
▸ indication of section(s) of work covered according to the specifications
▸ contract sum plus applicable federal, state, or provincial sales taxes (final total also to be included)
▸ reminder to contractor of requirements for performance bond and/or insurance as dictated in the terms of the general conditions
▸ distribution of copies: owner, contractor, appropriate consultants (if involved)
▸ authorizing signature of owner
▸ authorizing signature and seal of contractor

Proposed Change Notice

A proposed change notice or "PCN", is a form issued by the designer to the contractor, requesting prices for proposed changes to the specifications already agreed to in the owner/contractor contract. These changes are often an addition to, or a deletion from, the original items in the contract.

The proposed change notice should include:

- design firm: logo, name, address, telephone and fax numbers
- title of the form: *Proposed Change Notice*
- number of issue
- project name and address
- file number
- date
- name and address of contractor to whom the PCN is being issued
- specifications of items or work under consideration
- cautionary note, such as "Do not proceed with work affected by this Proposed Change Notice until authorized"
- distribution of copies: contractor, owner, appropriate consultants (if involved)
- signature

Change Order

The change order is a form issued to the contractor by the designer authorizing the contractor to proceed with approved changes to the original specifications as already agreed in the contract.

A change to the contract sum or contract time has been covered in the proposed change notice and agreed to by the owner.

The change order should include:

- design firm: logo, name, address, telephone and fax numbers
- title of the form: *Change Order*
- number of issue
- project name and address
- file number
- date
- name and address of contractor to whom the change order is being issued
- name of person sending the order
- specification of items or work to be changed
- distribution of copies: contractor, owner, appropriate consultants (if involved)
- authorizing signature of owner or designer (depending on arrangements)

Site Inspection Report

During the installation stage of the project, the designer makes periodic inspections of the site as agreed to in the client/designer contract.

The designer records the evaluation of the construction work covered under the contract documents and/or items delivered and installed as specified in the purchase order.

The site inspection report should include:

- design firm: logo, name, address, telephone and fax numbers
- title of the form: *Site Inspection Report*
- number of issue
- project name and address
- file number
- date of inspection
- date of report
- name of owner to whom the report is being sent
- name of person sending the report
- items inspected
- remarks
- distribution of copies: contractor(s), owner, appropriate consultants (if involved)
- signature

**Site Supervision
Order**

If, during a supervision visit to the project site, the designer decides that a change is required on the project, a written order may be issued *at that time, on site*. This order must be recorded and copies distributed to the contractor(s) and all other parties involved on the project.

If, in the opinion of the contractor(s), this order will require work, monies, or time that is additional to the contract, notice must be provided to the designer, in writing, prior to the work being performed and no later than three working days from receipt of the order.

The site supervision order should include:
- design firm: logo, name, address, telephone and fax numbers
- title of the form: *Site Supervision Order*
- number of issue
- project name and address
- file number
- date
- name of contractor(s) to whom the order is being issued
- name of person issuing order
- cautionary reminder to the contractor re: conditions of terms (see paragraph above)
- description of work to be modified
- distribution of copies: owner, contractor, appropriate consultants (if involved)
- authorizing signature

**Certificate for
Payment**

When all items or a sizable portion of the goods as specified in the purchase order have been delivered and installed on the project site, or when all or a portion of the construction work has been completed according to the construction specifications, the contractor may invoice all or a percentage of the monies owing. Terms of payment are outlined in the general conditions section of the furnishings specifications and the construction specifications. (The terms vary for these two types of specifications.)

The designer examines the invoice and usually makes an inspection. If everything is in order, the designer approves the invoice for payment.

The certificate for payment is a form issued to the owner recommending the amount to be paid to the contractor. It includes a statement of the status of the contract and a statement of payments, previous and current.

The certificate for payment includes:
- design firm: logo, name, address, telephone and fax numbers
- title of the form: *Certificate for Payment*
- number of issue
- project name and address
- file number
- date
- owner's name and address
- contractor's name and address
- statement of contract, including in dollar value:
  original contract
  total adjustments including change order numbers
  contract to date
  work done to date
  balance to complete

► statement of payments including:
>   work claimed for hold-back percentage
>   amount payable
>   previous certificate
>   this certificate
>   total of approved certificates
► design firm name and authorizing signature

Final Inspection Report

When the contractor claims that the project has been completed, a final inspection must be made by the designer, accompanied by a representative of the contractor and possibly a representative of the owner.

The final inspection report is a form issued by the designer listing all the items of the project and stating whether each item is complete or deficient.

The final inspection report includes:
► design firm: logo, name, address, telephone and fax numbers
► title of the form: *Final Inspection Report*
► project name and address
► file number
► date
► name of contractor(s) and person(s) to whom the report is issued
► names of participants in the final inspection
► items inspected
► indication of completeness or deficiency
► distribution of copies: owner, contractor(s), appropriate consultants (if involved)
► signature

Award of Contracts

Contracts for furnishings are awarded by the designer after bids are received, reviewed, recommended to the owner, and approved.

Contracts may take the form of purchase orders, or may be signed as contracts emanating from the supplier's bid. The owner is usually the signing authority in either case.

The designer/design firm is responsible for notifying unsuccessful bidders and for the return of bid deposits after the bidders have returned all specifications documents.

The Construction
Industry

11

As in every other industry, the construction business is made up of firms of all types: large and small, general and specialized, good and bad.

The industry is affected by many variables, such as the size of the community, the availability of labor and materials, and the state of the economy. Individual firms are usually well known in the whole built-environment industry as their past work, for the most part, is the basis for their reputation. Design firms often have favorite contractors they prefer to work with, yet realize that the size and budget of any one project may make a difference in the eventual choice of contractor.

During the course of any construction or renovation project, three basic factors must be considered:
▶ design intent
▶ cost control
▶ time schedule

Factors in the Construction Process

All actions planned or taken during the construction process will affect each of the these. The designer must always bear this in mind; any decision contemplated must be prefaced by the following considerations:
▶ How will this decision affect the design?
▶ What will this decision cost?
▶ What time will be saved or lost by this decision?

The major participants in the construction process include the designer, the general contractor, the subcontractor, consortiums, and building-materials suppliers.

Major Participants

In the construction process, the designer
▶ determines the work to be done, its scope and quality
▶ ensures that the project meets all standards required by the various jurisdictional authorities (depending on the type of project, approval may be necessary from municipal, provincial, state, or federal governments; fire protection authority; department of labor; department of health; liquor control authority)
▶ uses essential knowledge of the various codes (ignorance of the law is no excuse; even when a building permit has been issued, discovery of a code infraction may require conformation, thus necessitating changes in the design, greater expense and/or delay)
▶ specifies the quality and characteristics of products to be used
▶ describes in broad terms the methods of performing the work
▶ effects an agreement between the owner and the contractor that is equitable to both parties
▶ ensures that all parties are protected by applicable types of insurance

The Designer

▸ supervises construction to ensure that the work is
performed as designed and in accordance with appropriate
standards and codes
▸ manages the correct disbursement of all monies

**The General
Contractor**

In the construction process, the general contractor
▸ determines the scope of work required, assembles the
various trades and receives prices from
them, compiles these prices, adds on
costs plus mark-up for profit and supervision, and submits a total bid for the
project
▸ signs contract with the owner
▸ obtains the building permit (except for
plumbing and electrical work when
permits are obtained by the sub-
contractors)
▸ signs contracts with each sub-trade
▸ coordinates and supervises the various
trades hired to complete the specialized
tasks involved in the project
▸ carries appropriate insurance and
ensures that the sub-trades have
adequate insurance
▸ pays sub-trades (the client pays only the
general contractor)
▸ may provide certain services, such as
the project office, signage, hoarding,
cranes and hoists, temporary services,
clean-up and trash removal, and casual
labor

**The Sub-
Contractor**

In the construction process, sub-contractors
▸ specialize in particular trades
▸ submit bid prices to the general contractor
▸ provide material, equipment, and installation services
▸ carry appropriate insurance

Small Projects Not all projects are large enough to
warrant the use of a general contractor. With small projects
the designer may elect to deal with the sub-trades directly–in
effect acting as the general contractor.

For the protection of both the client and the designer, it
is important to follow the basic practices of the construction
industry, paying attention to such concerns as liens, compensation, adherence to codes, and so forth.

In fairly simple addition or renovation jobs, sub-trades
such as plumbing, heating, and electrical are usually capable
of doing the technical design. The sub-trade will work out the
necessary design with the designer, and then apply for the
permit.

"Home improvement" or generalist contractors can efficiently handle small jobs. They usually have a plumber and an
electrician on staff. Because their overhead costs are lower,
they are often more economical for a smaller project. The
designer must take care to ensure that such contractors are
reputable and financially sound.

Large Projects If a project is too large for one general
contractor, two or more may form a type of partnership, or

consortium, for the purpose of bidding. Sub-contractors may also form consortiums.

Construction
Specifications   127

In the construction process, building-materials suppliers

Building-Materials Suppliers

▶ supply catalogs, technical information, and test results
▶ give material and/or equipment prices to sub-contractors
▶ expedite deliveries of products
▶ in some cases, offer assistance in job supervision
▶ when providing a factory-produced item, may provide the sub-contractor with shop drawings

Construction specifications may be lettered or typed on drawing sheets, or contained in a specifications manual. These specifications are read in conjunction with working drawings. In the case of a discrepancy, the written specification takes precedence over the drawing.

Construction Specifications

Information should be given only once and should appear in the most logical place. All other locations in the contract documents where that same information might appear should simply make an explicit reference to the location where the information *is* shown.

Standard formats for specifications and other construction documents have been developed and are available from:

Specifications Format

▶ Construction Specifications Canada
Suite 1206–1 St. Clair Avenue West
Toronto, Ontario, M4V 1K6
Canada

▶ Construction Specifications Institute
601 Madison Street
Alexandria, Virginia 22314
U.S.A.

The numbering system and the order of sections in the CSC/CSI format has been adopted by building materials and equipment manufacturers and suppliers. The file numbers on their literature and in *Sweets Catalog* (a comprehensive listing of information from manufacturers) follow this system:

Sections
▶ 0   Building and Contract Requirements
▶ 1   General Data
▶ 2   Site Work
▶ 3   Concrete
▶ 4   Masonry
▶ 5   Metals
▶ 6   Wood and Plastics
▶ 7   Thermal and Moisture Protection
▶ 8   Doors and Windows
▶ 9   Finishes
▶ 10   Specialties
▶ 11   Equipment
▶ 12   Furnishings
▶ 13   Special Construction
▶ 14   Conveying Systems
▶ 15   Mechanical
▶ 16   Electrical

Construction Contracts

Construction contracts are a body of written documents used to protect all parties involved in the transaction. They should be fair to all participants and should cover all contingencies that might occur during the period of work.

In renovation projects, the wording of the contract is particularly important due to the possibility of unforeseeable conditions that could involve extra work and expense. Both the owner and the contractor need to be protected against such costs being incurred without their knowledge.

Construction contracts are written and agreement is obtained in order to
- clarify design intent, performance criteria, quality and characteristics of materials, and installation methods
- ensure that all aspects of construction meet government standards and codes
- define the parties involved and their areas of responsibility
- act as legal documents for the protection of all parties involved

Types of Contracts

Stipulated Price Contract A general contractor tenders a price on the project, including the bids received from all sub-trades. The contract is signed for *one total fixed sum* of money. To obtain the contract, contractors bid under the same conditions, and the successful tender is announced publicly.

Negotiated Contract The client and the contractor agree on an equitable system of handling the job, and negotiate prices on all materials and installations involved in the project. These negotiations are conducted in confidence and therefore the exact terms are not made common knowledge.

Segregated Contract This type of contract is sometimes used on small projects with no general contractor; instead, the designer or client's representative awards individual contracts to sub-contractors, co-ordinates the project, and administers all the separate contracts.

Construction Management Contract On very large projects, the client may retain a company to manage the project. This company coordinates the project and the contractors and does all of the administrative work involved.

Cost-Plus Contract The client agrees to pay the general contractor for all *costs plus a stipulated percentage* for profit. Sometimes a guaranteed maximum figure is included that ensures that the total cost to the client will not exceed that figure (and may be less).

Owner/Builder Contract This type of contract may be used where the owner (client), contractor, and, on occasion, a developer, jointly undertake a project. Each is part-owner and expects to derive income or profit from the investment. This motivates the parties involved to expedite the work in the best and most economical manner.

Sub-Contracts Sub-contracts are the contracts with those sub-trades involved on the project.

Progress Billing Since a construction project usually takes months–even years–to complete, it is necessary to pay the contractor progressively, usually on a monthly basis, in proportion to the amount of work completed at the time of billing.

Payment

This system is called *progress billing* and involves the following steps:
- The contractor submits a claim for payment to the designer.
- The designer determines if the claim is valid; if it is not (for example, when the work completed is unsatisfactory), the designer asks the contractor for further information or justification.
- When satisfied, the designer provides the client with a certificate for payment.
- Client pays the contractor.

Holdbacks It is normal procedure to withhold a certain amount of money, usually 10 percent, from each claim for payment in order to protect the client from defective workmanship, materials, or liens.

Only when everything is proven satisfactory, is this "holdback" released. Part of the holdback payment will be released upon completion of the project, with the balance held back until the final payment.

Liens On receipt of payment, the contractor usually issues a declaration that all sub-trades have been paid to date. This is in accordance with the contract documents, and protects the client from liens.

Various governmental jurisdictions have differing regulations regarding liens. Be sure to check the established practice carefully for each project.

Final Payment Final payment constitutes completion
and acceptance of the job, except for guarantees and warranties. By this action, the client and the contractor waive all
rights and claims against each other under the terms of the
contract.

Drawings, Schedules, and Shop Drawings

12

Drawings and schedules are produced to ensure that the interior designer's ideas are crystal clear, and that there is no doubt as to what the finished product is to be.

Schedules and drawings form a set of instructions. The main purpose is to establish a *simple* method of telling the contractor or sub-trade exactly what is wanted. Concise, simple, yet detailed instructions will save the designer and the firm time and trouble. Executors of the project should never have the opportunity to claim, "We don't understand your drawings or your schedules."

Preparation

Before beginning to produce a set of working drawings, schedules, or shop drawings (if you work for a manufacturer), the designer should ask the following questions:

▶ What does the project require?
▶ What instructions are needed?
▶ What is the simplest, most complete way of providing the instructions?
▶ What visual format will be most effective?
▶ What possible problems could arise and how could these drawings and schedules eliminate or lessen them?

**Working
Drawings**

For an interior project, a set of working drawings might include the following, usually in this order:

- interior space plan
- reflected ceiling plan
- electrical plan
- mechanical plan
- furnishings plan
- elevations
- sections
- details

Depending on the size of the project, some of the above may be combined, and for some projects the order of the drawings may be changed. For example, for a design of premises requiring a liquor license, the furnishings plan might be placed first, as the liquor license is the first to be obtained.

Working drawings should include

- all information, plans, elevations, sections, details, material indications, and notes that are necessary for standard and/ or custom construction
- materials information, provided both in words and with graphic illustration
- all necessary dimensions (if dimensions are approximate due to site conditions, then a plus or minus symbol should be used to indicate that a small variation will be allowed)
- major cardinal direction (north by custom at the top of the sheet)
- vertical grid lines, usually identified by numbers, and horizontal grid lines identified by letters (when building drawings include grid lines on the plan sheet)
- sheet numbers and drawing references indicating on which sheets elevations, sections, or details are located, and on which drawings on those sheets
- sufficient details to describe the work, but not so many as to confuse or insult the intelligence of the contractor
- a statement, often located below the title block, "Contractor to check all dimensions on site"

The importance of making clear and concise *written* additions, revisions, and deletions to specifications, drawings, and schedules cannot be overemphasized. To avoid confusion regarding changes, designers should never depend solely upon oral instructions for changes.

When revisions are made to working drawings *during* the tendering period, they are issued to the bidders as addenda (refer to page 119). When revisions occur *after* the owner/ contractor contract has been signed, they are issued as proposed change notices (refer to page 120).

**Related
Schedules**

Related schedules should contain enough information so that the general contractor knows what is involved, at which location, and who is responsible. These schedules will vary according to the complexity of the project and may include the following:

- room-finish schedule
- door schedule
- color schedule
- lighting schedule
- furnishings schedule

Different design firms publish their schedules in different forms. Some schedules, such as the room-finish schedule and the door schedule, are often located on the working drawings. Most schedules are typed on letter-size ($8^1/_2$" x 11") paper, less frequently on legal-size ($8^1/_2$" x 14") paper. (The furnishings schedule is generally in typed form.)

Numbering

In order to establish a schedule, all spaces need to be identified. Design offices' systems vary, but the general practice is that numbers–clear, concise, and easy-to-read–are assigned in the following patterns:

- all areas are numbered with numbers in sequence both horizontally and vertically
- doors are numbered in reference to the area *into which they swing*
- door numbers are located along doors so that they do not block entrances or interfere with other information

General Organization

When schedules are published, each document should be checked for the following:

Common Information
- design firm: logo, name, address, telephone and fax numbers
- name of the project
- project number/file number of the project
- job site and address
- date
- table of contents
- page numbers
- list of abbreviations

Format: information in logical sequence with
- headings for emphasis
- margins, indentations, columns
- allowance for binding
- good design
- continuity of schedules for the project

Organization of information so that the document can be issued to the pertinent tradesperson, artisan, or sales representative, and includes
- clear, concise, and easily referable information
- correct spelling
- correct indication of proper names
- good grammar

When schedules are located on working drawings, the same checklist generally applies. For finishes, symbols may be used instead of actual names. These symbols must be clear and developed in a way which leaves no doubt about their reference. A legend of symbols must be included.

Room-Finish Schedule

A room-finish schedule designates the materials and finishes to be applied to the building shell. It includes
- the name and number of the area
- flooring
- bases
- walls: north, east, south, west
- ceiling

‣ remarks and/or notes on additional work such as plastic laminates, millwork, stair details
‣ abbreviations and symbols

Door Schedule

A door schedule usually indicates the dimensions, style, material, finish, and sometimes color, as well as the location of all doors required for a project. It includes

‣ door:
    number
    nominal size
    type
    core
    finish
    UL label (Underwriters' Laboratories)
    material
‣ frame:
    type
    material
    finish
‣ hardware (this may be a separate schedule)
‣ remarks

Color Schedule

A color schedule may designate the color of all building materials used on a project, or may designate only the colors for the painting contractor.

The following information is included in a color schedule:

‣ name and number of the area
‣ flooring
‣ bases
‣ walls: north, east, south, west
‣ ceiling
‣ doors
‣ frames, mullions, trim
‣ remarks and/or notes on additional work such as plastic laminates, balustrades, handrails
‣ sources list
‣ abbreviations
‣ general notes

Some design firms list the type of coating and level of gloss by a coding system. Sometimes the room-finish schedule and the color schedule are combined.

Lighting Schedule

Lighting schedules list all the light fixtures specified in the contract which are to be supplied and installed by the electrical contractor. Portable floor and table lamps are usually included in the furnishings schedule.

The lighting schedule may be on the same drawing sheet as the reflected ceiling plan or on the following sheet. It is usually included in the working drawings rather than as a separate item.

The lighting schedule should include the following information:

‣ symbol: usually a shape similar to that of the fixture specified, accompanied by a lower-case letter code; for example, the symbol for a pot light would be a circle (note that lower-case lettering is used to distinguish coding from the traditional upper-case lettering of a working drawing)

- location: room name and/or number (a specific description such as "under overhead cupboards, in recessed cone" should appear under *remarks*)
- type: a description of the kind of fixture, such as "recessed incandescent" or "surface-mounted fluorescent"
- quantity: the number of fixtures of that type
- manufacturer's name: the name of the manufacturer or company that distributes the fixture
- catalog number: the correct code number from the manufacturer's catalog
- lamp: specification of the light source, such as, "MR 16, 75R40, F48 T12 CW"
- remarks: information regarding special finishes, special installation, hanging height, lens type, dimmer, or anything else that is non-standard about the fixture
- manufacturers and/or local distributors: names and addresses

Furnishings Schedule

The furnishings schedule is a list of all the furnishings required for a project. It serves as a room-by-room inventory of furniture and accessories, and sometimes includes window treatments and carpet. The schedule is developed from the design program, and is used in conjunction with the design development budget preparation. It becomes the basis for the furnishings specifications.

The furnishings schedule is generally published in a binder format, and includes the following:

- room number and name
- item name
- item number
- catalog number
- quantity
- description
- components as required:
    dimensions
    color
    material
    finish
    other information as required
- manufacturer or source
- suppliers' or manufacturers' names and addresses

Columns may be set aside for such elements as unit prices or extensions. The designer may wish to indicate the budget estlmate of each unil beside the description. The revised, completed furnishings schedule may be kept on file with the designer and with the client as an inventory document.

Shop Drawings

Shop drawings are graphic representations of the essential data for construction. They are required for custom work that must be carried out to the designer's intent. These drawings must be followed exactly by the shop doing the work. Shop drawings include expanded detail sheets for a particular item or other custom work.

Usually, the drawings are produced by the successful sub-contractor and sent to the designer by the manufacturer or supplier of that item for checking and approval. The written confirmation of approval becomes an official document. The designer must verify that the shop drawings represent *exactly* what is required, and should not authorize them unless they are accurate, with no changes to be made or errors to be corrected. Once a signature of approval is on these drawings, errors become the responsibility of the designer.

Shop Drawings Record

All shop drawings–submitted by the contractor for the designer's review and approval, for custom millwork, cabinetry, or other special items requiring approval of the designer–should be recorded throughout the project. However, there may be a person within the design firm or an outside consultant whose responsibility it is to check the drawings. The person approving the drawings should be identified on the record. The designer's written approval is required before the contractor may proceed.

The shop drawings record should include the following:
- design firm: logo, name, address, telephone and fax numbers
- title of the form: *Shop Drawings Record*
- project name and address
- file number
- name of contractor submitting drawings
- description of each set of shop drawings
- identification of person checking each set of shop drawings
- date of receipt of each set of drawings
- date of return of each set of drawings to the contractor
- action to be taken regarding drawings, such as *to be revised and resubmitted, approved as noted,* or *approved*

Conclusion

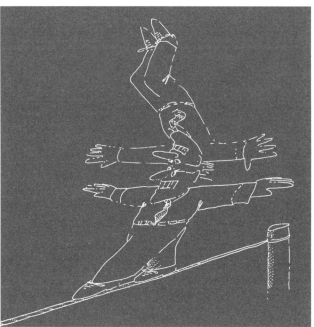

The new interior design graduate joins an established profession, a profession that is not moribund with age but vital and growing, and therefore in a state of flux. It is important for those entering the profession to understand the complexity of interior design and the subtle intermixture of disciplines involved in creating environments for all types of human habitation.

Interior design is an international profession which exemplifies the global village concept. Through local, national, and international involvement, each interior designer can develop a better understanding of the generic needs of people as well as the individual variances due to geography, climate, and culture.

To be recognized as a true profession, the business of interior design must be conducted in a professional manner. It is imperative that interior designers seek and heed the advice of consultants in the business world. Interior design is a service profession and, as with any service, it must be sold to the consumer. Successful interior designers pay considerable attention to the effective marketing of their skills and knowledge. An important aspect of the business management of a design firm is embodied in the contracts and fee systems. A legal and ethical stance must be maintained in all activities within the profession.

Success, both financial and creative, may depend to a great degree on the successful management of the project itself. Efficient use of skills and time is important but requires the effective use of the design process–beginning with in-depth programming and continuing with care and thought for the users–through to the evaluation of the completed work.

Efficiency also comes into play in the production of the working drawings, related schedules, and specifications. Careful attention to minute detail is required in this phase. Reputations and livelihood may be lost through careless errors.

The creation of the built environment requires teamwork, not only with related disciplines, but also with the construction industry. Knowledge of *how* things are built is an important aspect of designing things to be built. Much can be learned from the people who turn designs into reality.

The information in this book has been gathered together to provide a basis upon which the new interior designer may build. Being involved in the profession, both organizationally and in practice, and continuing to have a mind open to new development and growth will provide the rest.

Appendix

A Member of the American Society of Interior Designers is required to conduct his or her professional practice in a manner that will command the respect of clients, suppliers of goods and services to the profession, and fellow professional designers, as well as the general public. It is the individual responsibility of every member of the Society, both Professional and Associate, to observe and uphold this code and to maintain standards of professional and personal conduct that will reflect in a responsible manner on the Society and the profession.

The Code of Ethics of the ASID

▶ The designer shall conform to existing laws, regulations, and codes governing business procedures and the practice of interior design as established by the state or community in which he or she practices.

▶ The designer shall not engage in any form of false or misleading advertising or promotional activities and shall not imply, through advertising or other means, that staff members or employees of the firm are qualified interior designers unless such be the fact.

Responsibility to the Public

▶ The designer will, before entering into a contract either verbal or written, clearly determine the scope and nature of the project and the methods of compensation.

▶ The designer may offer professional services to the client as a consultant, specifier, and/or supplier on the basis of a fee, percentage, or mark-up.

▶ The designer shall have the responsibility of fully disclosing to the client the manner in which all compensation is to be paid. Unless the client knows and agrees, the designer is forbidden under this code to accept any form of compensation from a supplier of goods and services in cash or in kind.

▶ The designer shall perform services for the client in a manner consistent with the client's best interests, wishes, and preferences, so long as those interests, wishes, and preferences do not violate laws, regulations, and codes, or the designer's aesthetic judgment. The designer shall not divulge any privileged information about the client or the client's project, or utilize photographs or specifications of the project, without the express permission of the client, with an exception for those specifications or drawings over which the designer retains proprietary rights.

▶ The designer shall not present design work to the client that has not been prepared by a professional designer or prepared under the supervision of a professional designer.

Responsibility to the Client

▶ The designer shall not initiate any discussion or activity that might result in unjust injury to another professional designer's reputation or business relationships.

▶ The designer, when asked, may render a second opinion to a client, or may serve as an expert witness in a judicial proceeding.

Responsibility to Other Designers

- ▶ The designer shall not interfere with the performance of another designer's contractual arrangement with a client.
- ▶ The designer may enter into the design work on a project upon being personally satisfied that the client has severed contractual relationships with a previous designer.
- ▶ The designer shall only take credit for work that has actually been created by the designer or under the designer's direction.

Responsibility to the Society and the Profession

In accepting membership in the Society, the member agrees, whenever possible and within the scope of his or her interests and abilities, to encourage and contribute to the sharing of ideas and information between interior designers and other allied professional disciplines, as well as the industry that supplies goods and services to the profession; to offer support and encouragement to students of interior design and to those interested in the study of interior design, as well as those entering the profession; and to become involved in those community projects that enhance and improve the quality of life for all people.

Any deviation from this code, or from subsequent revisions of it by the Board of Directors of the American Society of Interior Designers, or any action detrimental to the Society and the profession as a whole, shall be deemed unprofessional conduct subject to discipline by the Society's Board of Directors.

The Code of Ethics and Professional Practice of Interior Designers of Canada

All members of the Interior Designers of Canada, undertake as a condition of their membership to abide by this Code of Ethics and Professional Practice:

- ▶ 1) A member will practice his or her profession by offering his or her knowledge, skill, and understanding in the solving of environmental, people, and space-related problems to members of the public and other professions.
- ▶ 2) A member will honestly and diligently represent his or her employer or client within the term of his or her engagement and as set out in the document "Outline of Services, Assessment of Fees, Code of Ethics" for the Interior Designers of Canada.
- ▶ 3) A member will not be party to any financial or other inducement in addition to his or her professional form of remuneration.
- ▶ 4) As a practicing member of the Interior Designers of Canada, a member will disclose in writing to his or her employer or client, prior to any engagement, any financial interest that he or she may have that could affect his or her impartiality in specifying goods and services.
- ▶ 5) A member, in the case of a dispute not involving him or her directly during his or her engagement on a project, will take an independent position in total fairness to the parties in dispute.
- ▶ 6) A member will treat his or her fellow designers with respect.
- ▶ 7) A member will not seek to supplant a fellow designer who is already engaged on a project.
- ▶ 8) A member will, in competition with other designers, seek his or her engagement only through his or her knowledge, skill, and understanding and by observing highest professional ethics.

▶ 9) A member will not knowingly plagiarize the design of another designer.

▶ 10) Notice of contravention of the above ethical standards must be made in writing to the relevant constituent association of the IDC. A member found in contravention of this Code of Ethics will submit to the ruling of the authority designated by the relevant constituent association of the IDC.

▶ 11) A member will at all times give his or her professional best to be a worthy member of the Interior Designers of Canada.

Bibliography

▸ Alderman, Robert L. *How to Make More Money at Interior Design.* New York: Whitney Communications, 1982.

▸ Bormann, Ernest G., and Nancy C. Bormann. *Speech Communication: An Interpersonal Approach.* New York: Harper and Row Publishers, 1972.

▸ Davis, Gerald, and Francoise Sziegeti. *Functional Programming for Facilities: What It Is, Why It Is Needed, Who Does It, and When.* Ottawa, Ontario, lecture paper, 1978.

▸ Deasy, C. M. *Designing Places for People.* New York: Whitney Library of Design, 1985.

▸ Hardie, Glenn M. *Construction Contracts and Specifications.* Reston, VA: Reston Publishing Company, 1981.

▸ Harrigan, John E., and Janet R. Harrigan. *Human Factors Program for Architects, Interior Designers and Clients.* San Luis Obispo, CA: Blake Printing and Publishing, 1976.

▸ Jones, Gerre. *How to Market Professional Design Services.* 2nd ed. New York: McGraw-Hill, 1983.

▸ Knackstedt, Mary V. *Interior Design for Profit.* New York: Kobro Publications, 1980.

▸ Knackstedt, Mary V., with Laura J. Haney. *The Interior Design Business Handbook.* New York: Whitney Library of Design, 1988.

▸ Loebelson, Andrew. *How To Profit in Contract Design.* New York: Whitney Communications, 1983.

▸ Morgan, Jim. *Marketing for the Small Design Firm.* New York: Whitney Library of Design, 1984.

▸ Morris, John O. *Make Yourself Clear.* New York: McGraw-Hill, 1972.

▸ Preiser, Wolfgang. *Facility Programming: Methods and Applications.* Stroudsburg, PA: Dowden, Hutchinson and Ross, 1978.

▸ Proshansky, Harold M., William H. Ittleson and Leanne G. Rivlin. *Environmental Psychology.* New York: Holt, Rinehart and Winston, 1970.

▸ Reznikoff, S. *Specifications for Commercial Interiors.* New York: Whitney Library of Design, 1979.

▸ Sanoff, Henry. *Methods of Architectural Programming.* Stroudsburg, PA: Dowden, Hutchinson and Ross, 1977.

► Siegel, Harry, with Alan Siegel. *A Guide to Business Principles and Practices for Interior Designers.* New York: Whitney Library of Design, 1982.

► Stitt, Fred A., ed. *Design Office Management Handbook.* Santa Monica: Arts & Architecture Press, 1986.

► Studer, Raymond, and David Stea. "Architectural Programming, Environmental Design, and Human Behavior." *The Journal of Social Issues*, Vol. 22, no. 4.

► Tate, A., and C. Smith. *Interior Design in the 20th Century.* New York: Harper and Row Publishers, 1987.